D1536581

SO OLDHAM

OCT 3 0 2018

CARD

The Big Book of Dyslexia
Activities for Kids and Teens

by the same author

Dyslexia in the Early Years
A Handbook for Practice
Gavin Reid
ISBN 978 1 78592 065 3
eISBN 978 1 78450 327 7

of related interest

Fun Games and Activities for Children with Dyslexia
How to Learn Smarter with a Dyslexic Brain
Alais Winton
Illustrated by Joe Salerno
ISBN 978 1 78592 292 3
eISBN 978 1 78450 596 7

Dyslexia is My Superpower (Most of the Time)
Margaret Rooke
Forewords by Professor Catherine Drennan and Loyle Carner
ISBN 978 1 78592 299 2
eISBN 978 1 78450 606 3

The Illustrated Guide to Dyslexia and Its Amazing People
Kate Power and Kathy Iwanczak
Foreword by Richard Rogers
ISBN 978 1 78592 330 2
eISBN 978 1 78450 647 6

Can I tell you about Dyslexia?
A guide for friends, family and professionals
Alan M. Hultquist
Illustrated by Bill Tulp
ISBN 978 1 84905 952 7
eISBN 978 0 85700 810 7

Specific Learning Difficulties – What Teachers Need to Know
Diana Hudson
Illustrated by Jon English
ISBN 978 1 84905 590 1
eISBN 978 1 78450 046 7

101 Inclusive and SEN English Lessons
Fun Activities and Lesson Plans for Children Aged 3–11
Kate Bradley and Claire Brewer
ISBN 978 1 78592 365 4
eISBN 978 1 78450 708 4

An Introduction to Dyslexia for Parents and Professionals
Alan M. Hultquist
ISBN 978 1 84310 833 7
eISBN 978 1 84642 527 1

I Don't Like Reading
Lisabeth Emlyn Clark
ISBN 978 1 78592 354 8
eISBN 978 1 78450 693 3

The Big Book of Dyslexia Activities for Kids and Teens

100+ Creative, Fun, Multi-sensory and Inclusive Ideas for Successful Learning

GAVIN REID, NICK GUISE AND JENNIE GUISE

Jessica Kingsley *Publishers*
London and Philadelphia

OLDHAM COUNTY PUBLIC LIBRARY
308 YAGER AVENUE
LAGRANGE, KY 40031

Image of golden syrup on page 31 is reproduced with kind permission of Tate & Lyle.
Image of Tunnock's wrappers on page 75 is reproduced with kind permission from Thomas Tunnock Ltd.

First published in 2018
by Jessica Kingsley Publishers
73 Collier Street
London N1 9BE, UK
and
400 Market Street, Suite 400
Philadelphia, PA 19106, USA

www.jkp.com

Copyright © Gavin Reid, Nick Guise and Jennie Guise 2018

All rights reserved. No part of this publication may be reproduced in any material form (including photocopying, storing in any medium by electronic means or transmitting) without the written permission of the copyright owner except in accordance with the provisions of the law or under terms of a licence issued in the UK by the Copyright Licensing Agency Ltd. www.cla.co.uk or in overseas territories by the relevant reproduction rights organisation, for details see www.ifrro.org. Applications for the copyright owner's written permission to reproduce any part of this publication should be addressed to the publisher.

Warning: The doing of an unauthorised act in relation to a copyright work may result in both a civil claim for damages and criminal prosecution.

Library of Congress Cataloging in Publication Data
A CIP catalog record for this book is available from the Library of Congress

British Library Cataloguing in Publication Data
A CIP catalogue record for this book is available from the British Library

ISBN 978 1 78592 377 7
eISBN 978 1 78450 725 1

Printed and bound in the United States

Contents

Acknowledgements   8

Introduction   9

Part 1: Literacy   **17**

Section 1: Reading   19

Music and Lyrics 20 · Nato Phonetic Alphabet 22 · Letters, Words
and Sentences 25 · All about the Horse 27 · Reading for Purpose 30 ·
Genre 32 · Information Leaflet 35

Section 2: Spelling   39

Spelling Corks 40 · Spelling Golf 42 · Spelling Ping-Pong 44 · Spelling
– Be a Teacher 46 · Target Words and Visual Connections 49 · Syllables,
Syllables, Syllables 51

Section 3: Written Expression   55

Churchill 56 · Frame It 60 · Snippets and More 62 · Be a Script Writer
64 · Creative Writing Pockets 66 · Rubber Band – A Writing Prompt 68 ·
Bananas 71 · Tunnock's Teacake 73 · VCOP (Vocabulary, Connectives,
Openers, Punctuation) 76 · Local Language 78 · Forest Walk 80

Section 4: Vocabulary   83

'A' is for... 84 · Poetry Path 85 · Word Wheel 88 · Nouns –
Flashcards 90 · Taste Texts 92 · Keys 94 · Tongue Twisters 97

Part 2: Learning   **101**

Section 5: General Knowledge   105

Pirates 106 · UFOs (Unidentified Flying Objects) 109 · Yellow 111 ·
Black 115 · Dodo 118 · Trees 121 · Water 125 · Circus 128 · Sweets 131 ·
Stunts 134

Section 6: Comprehension 139

What's New/Interesting/Forgettable? 140 · Time 142 · Volcanoes 145 · Critical Thinking 148 · Celebrity 'Mastermind' 152

Section 7: Learning Games for Fun 155

Pictures Say 100 Words 156 · Share for Success – 'Helping Me, Helping You' 157 · We've Got Talent 159 · Self-Portrait 162 · Quizzes 164 · Superstitions 167

Section 8: Memory 171

List the Lists 172 · Kim's Game 174 · Picture Card Prompts 176 · Pelmanism 178 · The Kluge 181 · Smells 184

Part 3: Cross-Curricular 189

Section 9: Number Work 191

Ellipse 192 · Framing 194 · Visual Spatial 197 · Armchair Olympics 200 · City Trip 203 · Overseas Trip 205 · Design a Den 208

Section 10: Including English as an Additional Language (EAL) 211

Adjective Wall 212 · PT (Position and Time) Prepositions 214 · Use My Name 217 · Verbs Charade 219 · Who Am I? 221 · Culture and Customs 223 · Idioms 226 · Opposites 229 · Diamante Poetry 231

Section 11: Different Curricular Areas 235

What We Eat 236 · Dewey Decimal System 238 · Spinneracy 241 · Using the Whole Brain 243 · Badge-Making 245 · Questioning Questions 247 · Sounds 251 · FreeRice 253 · Annotation 256 · Knots 258 · Film 260

Section 12: Creativity and Technology 263

Animation 264 · Inspiration 266 · Book Create 270 · Film Create 271 · Green Screen 273 · iTunes 274 · Review the Apps 275 · Birds 278 · Summaries 280 · Metal 282 · Telephone/Mobile 285

Section 13: Home and School 289

Shades of Colours 290 · North, South, East, West 292 · Which Way? 294 · Metro Paper 297 · Just Breathe 300

Appendix 1: Dewey Decimal Numbers   302

Appendix 2: Vocabulary Used in Activities   306

References   315

Index   316

About the Authors   320

Acknowledgements

The authors would like to acknowledge the kids and teens who provided the inspiration for the activities in this book, and for feedback that we received when using these activities. Additionally, friends and colleagues have been of great support, particularly Jenn Clark.

Introduction

We appreciate that there are a number of books on dyslexia available for facilitators. Many of these require a great deal of reading and studying before the ideas and approaches suggested can be implemented. Nevertheless, all books on dyslexia have an important function, particularly since there are now more opportunities for staff development and advanced university courses in this area.

We are, however, of the view – gained through experience and a great deal of discussion with teachers – that a relevant and practical 'ready to use' book would be extremely helpful. This is what we aim to achieve in our book. All the ideas and strategies have been tried and tested in the classroom, and have been developed in relation to the challenges faced by children and young people with dyslexia, in the learning context.

This book therefore provides whole-group activities that are specifically created with the dyslexic child in mind. The activities can be used in different settings such as traditional schools, specialist schools, home schooling or with small groups in mainstream schools.

The materials are 'dyslexia friendly' and they will benefit all children. Classroom teachers, specialist and learning support teachers, parents, tutors, SENCos and other support staff, regardless of where they are in the world, will be able to use the activities in this book.

We appreciate the increasingly vast workload and the time required to develop new ideas and strategies for effective intervention. In many ways, this perspective has provided the rationale for this book and we have sought to make the activities practical and ready to use in the classroom or home.

What Works Best

The premise for the activities in the book is based on the acknowledged wisdom of 'what works best' for learners with dyslexia. This includes structured, engaging and multi-sensory activities, and we have tried to incorporate these aspects into each of the activities. Additionally, the book has built in a number of overlearning activities and we have attempted to cross-reference these when one particular activity might be seen as overlearning for another. It is acknowledged that overlearning is essential for children with dyslexia. Overlearning can lead to automaticity, and if a child can perform tasks with automaticity, this means that the new learning has been consolidated. This can also lead to consistency, and we find that inconsistency is one of the frustrating issues experienced by children with dyslexia. Overlearning is therefore crucial. Overlearning is *not* rote repetition, but rather it relates to presenting materials or tasks that *reinforce* the same principles, rules or meaning as something that has been previously learned.

We are also aware that children with dyslexia can have short-term and long-term memory problems, as well as difficulties with processing information at speed. We have therefore included a section of activities dedicated to memory, and have developed a range of memory strategies that can be readily used by the young person with dyslexia. Several sections of the book are also dedicated to spelling and expressive writing. It is extremely frustrating for the child with dyslexia to have an abundance of ideas, but be unable to transfer these into coherent and expressive written language.

Additionally, we feel that children and young people with dyslexia also need to be 'stretched', and this includes using creativity and their imagination to promote thinking 'outside the box'. We have formulated a structured framework in all the activities so that facilitators can implement them more easily (see 'How to use this book' in this introduction). In addition to developing activities to help with different areas of learning, we have included opportunities to develop the young person's vocabulary and grammatical awareness. This is flagged in every activity, and each has a component on grammar and the vocabulary associated with the activity.

Barriers to Learning

As researchers, practitioners and psychologists, we are aware of the cognitive, social, emotional, educational and environmental barriers that confront children with dyslexia. This includes cognitive barriers such as difficulties with information processing, phonological processing, working memory, sequencing difficulties, spatial awareness and coordination difficulties and executive functioning difficulties, as well as organisational and time-keeping difficulties. Although not all children with dyslexia will experience all of these barriers, many will.

The social and emotional barriers can include lack of confidence, low self-esteem, isolation, anxiety and stress and learned helplessness due to a history of failure. These factors are dealt with in many of the activities, and the activities have been developed in a manner that can induce and promote success. This can offer a significant boost to children with dyslexia, thereby enhancing their self-esteem.

When looking at the barriers experienced by learners with dyslexia, we also need to consider factors within the educational environment. These can include the literacy demands placed on the child, lack of visual aids/prompts, unnecesary time pressures, peer and social expectations and limited access to technology. We have been very aware of these barriers, as well as all the other potential challenges faced by children with dyslexia, in creating and developing the activities. They will help to engage the child and make learning fun and successful.

Dyslexia is a learning difference, and children with dyslexia will often learn in a different way. We have introduced a new type of activity called 'Red Herrings' (see 'How to use this book') that can help to turn these 'differences' into more individual and successful reponses to a task. Learners with dyslexia have been metaphorically described as being able to 'see the unseen' (West 2017), and the implication of this for the children is that we need to encourage creativity, ingenuity and reponsibility.

One of the potentially confusing aspects about dyslexia is that it is not a discrete and narrow syndrome, and may be difficult to identify, and unfortunately many children are not identified until later in their education. The activities in this book will help those children who have the characteristics of dyslexia, but are not yet formally identified. This may be a significantly larger group than one might imagine!

The Whole Curriculum

The difficulties associated with dyslexia can have an impact across the whole curriculum – aspects such as remembering instructions, noting homework, reading, writing and spelling, sequencing information and organising notes and planning work can be crucial for every subject, including some of the practical subjects. For that reason, this book provides activities that deal with a wide range of curriculum areas. As well as sections on literacy, we have included general knowledge and general science, memory, number work, technology, cross-curricular activities and additional language learning.

This will make it more useful for users – rather than take a narrow approach, we have taken a broad, wider-angle approach to dyslexia, acknowledging the learning differences that can be seen within the dyslexic population. We believe that the activities represent effective and engaging learning. We also recognise that learner independence is important, and we have always encouraged learners to develop their own strategies and become more self-sufficient and independent. This way, they can further their own creative, investigative and learning skills, and in particular share learning experiences with peers.

Facilitators will be able to use the activities in this book immediately; they will also be able to develop and contextualise some to suit their programmes and curriculum needs.

This book has been the fruits of working with children and young people, as well as with teachers. Nick Guise has created many of the activities for use in his own classroom, and all the activities have been successfully tried and tested. The book will enrich the practice and enhance the learning needs of children with dyslexia.

How to Use this Book

This part of the introduction will explain how to use this book, and how the activities are formulated and arranged. All the activities have been tried and tested with children with dyslexia. They have also been developed for a wide range of ages, from early years to senior students.

We have divided the book into three main parts – Literacy, Learning and Cross-Curricular. Each of the parts is quite broad in scope. Part 1, Literacy, includes reading, spelling, written expression, vocabulary and grammar. Literacy difficulties represent the main hurdle experienced by children and young people with dyslexia, and these can often be long-standing, because there is no quick fix for dyslexia. We have acknowledged that children learn best when the task is fun, relevant and fits in with the existing everyday schema of their life. We have also encouraged children to find out for themselves, and thereby develop investigative skills. This also involves reading, spelling and writing, and therefore the activities in this part will help them develop literacy skills. These, particularly vocabulary, will be built up and extended as they go through the rest of the activities in the book.

Part 2, Learning, was included because learning skills are essential for the child with dyslexia, and can have an impact on all aspects of the curriculum. Although they may have a great deal of ability, they may have difficulty in engaging in the learning process and developing learning skills. This part includes memory, learning games, comprehension and general knowledge, including general science.

Part 3, Cross-Curricular, is on different curricular areas, and this includes activities that can cross curricular boundaries. This part includes number work, EAL (English as an Additional Language), music, games that reinforce skills that can be used throughout the whole curriculum, creativity and technology. We have also included at the end of this book a section on home and school. We appreciate the key role that parents play in their child's education wherever they are schooled, and we have included some tailored 'try this at home' type of activities here.

Format

You will find each activity starts with a short introduction to set the context for the activity. This includes the aims and rationale for the activity. This will include recognition of the skills that are seen as useful, and perhaps essential, for learners with dyslexia. Most of the activities will have a slightly different aim.

For continuity and consistency, and to promote overlearning, we have presented each activity in a uniform format, and this is described below.

Title of Activity

Each activity has an inherent importance, and the key point is that the user can select the activities accordingly. We have given each a title – some of them are self-explanatory; others will become clear once the introduction to the activity is read.

Requirements

Every activity will have a list of requirements. We have tried to make the activities simple and manageable for all facilitators, irrespective of the facilities on hand. Access to the internet is helpful and can be used in many activities, often as a follow-up. Each activity will have clear instructions. We have also provided some choices, so that the materials can be used flexibly, and if some of the materials noted in the activity are not available for the facilitator, there will be ideas and opportunities for improvisation.

Grammar

If you were to say to a group of learners, 'OK, today we are going to do grammar', the reaction would likely be an echo of groans and moans! But if the grammar is embedded into a visually appealing and exciting activity, it can be tackled almost unnoticed. We have inserted a grammar component into every activity, so it can become almost routine to tackle this within the activity.

The acronym VANs describes Verbs, Adjectives and Nouns. Every activity will have an example of a verb, adjective and noun associated with the activity. This will help to develop grammar skills and provide the opportunity to discuss these at the start of each activity. Certainly, by the end of the book every child will have a good idea of a verb, adjective and noun!

To avoid repetitiveness, we have not used the acronym in each activity, but we strongly suggest that you familiarise the child with this acronym when they are tackling the grammar part of the activity.

Vocabulary Development

In addition to the grammar aspect of each activity, there will also be opportunities to develop vocabulary. Each activity will have a list of associated words or key words that can be discussed during the activity or prior to the activity. We have suggested words for this, but you can, of course, add some of your own – particularly if the group has recently come across a word relevant to the activity that you may want to reinforce.

As a follow-through to enhance overlearning, Appendix 2 at the end of the book includes a list of the key words for each activity. This appendix can also be used as a revision exercise.

Main Activity

This will be clearly marked in each activity. It can take a number of forms, but we have tried to include background details about the topic and often a comprehension passage too. Again, although the activity is ready to use, it can be adapted to suit whatever needs.

Optional Activities

For most of the activities, we have provided optional additional activities. These will also take the form of overlearning, and can be stimulating and interesting for the child to complete. They can also be completed as a homework activity.

Red Herrings

One of the unique features of the book is the red herring! This idea was developed in classroom practice and has been found to strike a chord with the children.

Red herrings refer to what might be seen as 'going off at a tangent'. This, in fact, is quite common for children with dyslexia, and they are often encouraged not to do this and are told to keep to the question or point. Yet this tangential thinking can be extremely rich in creativity and ideas, and can lead to deeper thinking and extend the learning process, and indeed the skills of the learner with dyslexia. We therefore encourage this tangential thinking through the inclusion of 'red herrings' in many of the activities.

Red herrings can also be used as a means to involve individuals and groups who might otherwise be reluctant or reserved about participating in and discussing some topics. Many activities start off with a specific aim or goal, but allow scope for deviation from the core matter – red herrings are an ideal platform for this. The strands of connectivity with the core area of study/focus can be used to explore language and discussion in an inclusive way. The red herrings can be unpredictable, but the child's enjoyment can be enhanced by this unpredictability, and even if often they veer off to a totally unrelated topic, the level of talking and listening can be enhanced, and consequently the learning skills and outcomes improved.

The confidence of many individuals can develop as areas of personal experience often enter into the discussions. This engagement and interaction can be exciting, and what may appear to be not too appealing at first can develop into exciting and creative ideas. When a red herring does not appear in an activity, we urge the facilitator to either make one up, or, better still, ask the child to make one up! This would mean that the red herring would make an automatic appearance in every activity.

Activity Resources

We have also suggested some additional follow-up resources at the end of each activity in the form of websites.

Dewey Decimal

The Dewey Decimal system is the established and uniform system used universally for locating books in libraries. Each book is coded with a Dewey Decimal number, depending on the subject. This includes general headings such as philosophy, religion, social sciences, languages, science, maths, technology, arts, literature, geography and history. Each of these headings has a general number code, which can direct the child to the correct section in the library. Each general heading also has a specific subject-related code.

The Dewey Decimal system has been included in this book because it represents good practice for a learner with dyslexia. It involves reading skills, memory, writing, scanning and focusing skills. It also enhances independence.

Each activity will therefore have the number according to the Dewey list – for example, the activity 'Rubber Bands' has the Dewey Decimal code 'DD 730', which is 'Origami Paper Crafts'. The full Dewey Decimal list will be located in Appendix 1, and there is also an activity on Dewey Decimal in Section 11, 'Different Curricular Areas'.

Framework for Each Activity

We have presented each activity in the same format. This will help you use the activity more effectively. It will also promote overlearning, and additionally provide the child with an idea of how to tackle the activity, particularly as they become familiar with the terms and format.

Also, throughout the book we have tried to promote independence; having a uniform format helps with this, as it gives the child a degree of familiarity, even though all the activities will have a different focus. The specific format for each activity is shown below:

Activity Format

Title

Introduction/Aims

Requirements

Vocabulary

Associated Words

Main Activity

Optional Activity (if appropriate)

Red Herrings

We have also included some websites and the Dewey Decimal catalogue number when appropriate. Some of the activities do not have an optional activity – we feel this is a good opportunity for the teacher or the children to make up their own one – perhaps related to the work they are doing in class at that time.

Although the activities are arranged in sections, it is not necessary to work through the book sequentially. You can pick and choose, and even develop some of the ideas and activities in the book. We also see this as one of the purposes of the book. It can be core resource, a springboard for ideas, a dip-in activity book, a follow-up to lessons and a source of learning, fun and pleasure for the child.

Part 1

Literacy

Introduction

This first part of the book focuses on literacy because literacy difficulties usually present the biggest and most enduring challenge for children with dyslexia. In Part 1, the activities are divided into sections on reading, spelling, written expression and vocabulary expansion/grammar. This comprises more than 30 activities, and each uses the same format as discussed in the introduction to the book. This includes introducing new vocabulary and relating this to the activity.

In relation to reading, we would like to emphasise that reading is not only about 'cracking the code'! Certainly, the fundamentals of early reading skills are important, but reading is also about reading for meaning and obtaining pleasure from books! Additionally, reading will extend the learner's vocabulary and accompanying comprehension – paving the way for higher-order thinking skills. In many ways, therefore, reading can unlock the door for more effective and successful learning for the child with dyslexia. The experience of print is crucial, and we have acknowledged this in the activities in the reading section – for example, Reading for Purpose.

We are also aware that reading needs to be exciting, and we have an activity called Genre to help the child realise there is a wide choice out there, and that reading materials can be varied. The idea is to capture an area that will relate to the reader's interests. This is essential to effectively engage the child to read, because he/she *wants* to read, not because they have to!

There is also a section on spelling – not surprisingly, because spelling is often a major obstacle for children (and adults) with dyslexia. Luckily, we now have ready access to spell checkers, including some very sophisticated ones (e.g. the spell checker in Texthelp Read and Write Gold™) that are specifically developed with the learner with dyslexia in mind.

Certainly, spelling rules and patterns need to be learned, but these are best learned in context and not in isolation. Spelling can therefore be successfully embedded into learning for those children who have super ideas but are unwilling to get these down on paper because of spelling difficulties. It is important to emphasise that in some circumstances – for example, when engaging in creative writing – spelling does not matter. The spelling and writing activities in this book can be used to develop fluency and in a game format that gives the child a set time to complete the task. At the same time, you do not want to put more pressure on the child, so this should be carried out as a fun activity. Some of the activities in the spelling section are indeed fun activities – for example, Spelling Corks, Spelling Golf and Spelling Ping-Pong.

This part includes a range of activities on written expression. The emphasis here is on creativity and imagination. Often children with dyslexia have difficulties putting pen to paper, so this is a very important section. You can also permit the activities to be spoken rather than written, if the child is unable to fulfil the task in written form.

The activities in this section are engaging and varied. Many are unusual and have a practical and amusing twist – for example, Tunnock's Teacake, Local Language and Forest Walk.

Children with dyslexia can often experience vocabulary issues. They may know the word and its meaning but be unable to locate it when they need it! This type of word-finding difficulty is very characteristic of dyslexia. The section on vocabulary promotes the use of a wider vocabulary, thus making it possible for the child to use these words in a writing exercise. This section also includes grammar, although grammar is noted in every activity. Indeed, all activities in every section also promote learning and being able to use a wider vocabulary. More than 600 vocabulary words and their meanings are introduced in the vocabulary part of the activities throughout the book.

Enjoyment and engagement are the keys to successful learning. These factors have been uppermost on our minds throughout the development of this book so that reading and literacy in general can become not only a pleasure but also a successful activity for all children with dyslexia.

Reading

1 Music and Lyrics

Rhyming and rhythm are important for learning to read. This helps to enhance the child's awareness of sounds. Exercises to develop awareness of sounds and identifying similar and different sounds are important. This fits into the research on phonological awareness, which is seen as a key factor in learning to read, and difficulties in this area are associated with dyslexia.

The aim of this activity is to develop access to the sounds that make up words and specifically the use of rhyming words and phrases. This exercise can also help with memory, and the retention of sounds is made easier by the association with songs and music. This activity can also help to develop collaborative group work and team building.

Requirements

- pencils
- paper
- computer with access to internet (optional)
- microphone (optional – this can add a touch of professionalism and fun to the activity)

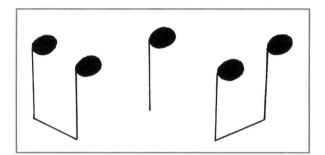

Vocabulary

Verb: compose

Adjective: tuneful

Noun: musician

Associated Words

Word	Meaning and example
orchestra	
stanza	
couplet	

lyrics	
composer	
arrangement	

Main Activity

1. Write a list of themes (see the themes below as an example, or make up your own) on to separate cards – one card for each theme.

2. Shuffle the pack. Each group has to choose one theme.

3. Each group has to write two verses of a song based on that theme. Use the internet to get some ideas on how to write a song.

4. As a prompt, play the first line of a well-known tune or song – this can give them ideas of a tune for the song.

5. Set the timer – give them 15 minutes.

6. Each group has to perform their song to the others. Ask each group to give their group an original and imaginative name. They should also give their song a name.

7. Nominate one member of the group to introduce the song.

Some suggested general themes (it might be a good idea to relate some of the themes to topic work the groups are currently working on):

- nursery rhymes
- movies
- sports
- romance
- school
- homework.

Optional Activity

Children can do the same activity, but this time they have a free choice over the theme. Importantly, they have to relate what the song means, and why it is a worthy theme for a song.

Have the children watch the movie *Music and Lyrics*. Then, ask them to write a summary of the story. Although it is a comedy, there is a serious message to this. Can you make a comment on 'life in the music business'?

Red Herring

This is a chance to analyse what makes a good song. Look at some of the clips from *The X Factor* or *American Idol* and note the judges' comments. Make a list of what judges look for in evaluating a song. Try to order your list 1–10.

Tip

Try not to make the activity competitive – we want everyone to feel they can give it a go.

Websites

Music and Lyrics (film) – at https://en.wikipedia.org

How to write a song: Ten songwriting tips from the pros – at www.dittomusic.com

How to write a song: Top ten tips – at www.youtube.com

Dewey Decimal

781

2 Nato Phonetic Alphabet

Children with dyslexia, even once they start reading, can still have a problem with sequencing. They may still confuse the order of letters or numbers further on in their learning, even though they have become more accomplished readers. For beginning readers, sequencing can be very problematic. They may get the order of letters or words mixed up, and even older children with dyslexia can have difficulty in sequencing an essay and arranging the paragraphs in an appropriate order. In addition to this, they usually have problems with memory, and this can make remembering sequences more challenging.

The aim of this activity is to develop and support learning and retain the sequential order of an alphabet, as well as memory development and reinforcement.

Requirements

- NATO phonetic alphabet cards (described below)
- computer and access to the internet (optional)

Vocabulary

Verbs: memorise, verbalise

Adjective: colourful

Noun: alphabet

Associated Words

Word	Meaning and example
sequence	
memorable	
vocalise	
association	
North Atlantic Treaty Organization (NATO)	

Main Activity

First, you should prepare NATO phonetic word cards such as those below.

Card 1	Card 2
ABC	A – Alpha B – Bravo C – Charlie
DEF	D – Delta E – Echo F – Foxtrot

GHI	G – Golf H – Hotel I – India
JKL	J – Juliet K – Kilo L – Lima
MNO	M – Mike N – November O – Oscar
PQR	P – Papa Q – Quebec R – Romeo
STU	S – Sierra T – Tango U – Uniform
VWX	V – Victor W – Whiskey X – Xray
YZ	Y – Yankee Z – Zulu

You should prepare the cards well in advance of the activity. Once you have Card 1 prepared, ask the children to read one letter at a time from A to Z. This can be done as a group activity so the children can read in turns until the whole alphabet is complete.

The next step is for them to read three letters at once as per Card 1 above. This can be done a number of times for overlearning.

Introduce the terms associated with each letter – Card 2. You may want to get some TV clips – for example, from police programmes where the terms are used in communication.

Ask each group to remember one set of the three terms used in Card 2 – they can also integrate actions into this activity. This can be a fun activity, and eventually the aim is for all groups to be able to memorise all the terms and the sequence of the alphabet. This can also be a good memory exercise for older children.

Optional Activity

The NATO phonetic alphabet is commonly used today in police dramas. It first became popular in a police drama series called *Z Cars* in the 1960s. Watch some YouTube clips of this series. Make a list of the changes in police work since that programme was made. Make a list of the good and not so good points.

Red Herring

Encourage discussion using any of the words in the NATO phonetic alphabet – for example, 'Romeo' and 'Juliet'. They can use mimes (e.g. hand on heart for Romeo/Juliet, golf swing for Golf, microphone for Mike) and any of the words to prompt memory.

Websites

How was Nato's phonetic alphabet chosen? – at www.theweek.co.uk

NATO phonetic alphabet – at https://en.wikipedia.org

Dewey Decimal

470, 471

3 Letters, Words and Sentences

Children with dyslexia require a great deal of overlearning. This helps them acquire automaticity, which is important to be able to transfer learning from one context to another. This is vital for reading, as it means the child will be able to acquire the use of rules and conventions for reading, and also use contextual and semantic cues. It is important to use activities that can develop sounds and word manipulation. This means that the child will be able to recognise the same word endings or syllables in different words or phrases in sentences that follow a pattern.

This activity can be tailored to different ages – for young children the aim is to develop alphabet knowledge and alliteration, so they can recognise the sounds that groups of letters make. For older children, this can be phrases or several phrases that often mean the same thing. Letter, word and phrase familiarity and manipulation are good exercises for reading. For example, games such as Scrabble do exactly this; this activity is similar to Scrabble.

Vocabulary

Verb: construct

Adjective: grammatical

Noun: phrase

Associated Words

Word	Meaning and example
listen	
sound	
rhyme	
sense	

Main Activity

1. Make cut-out cards of all the letters of the alphabet.

2. Place each of the letter cards in a bag and shuffle them.

3. Arrange the children into pairs.

4. Each pair has to pick one letter from the bag.

5. The whole group together then says the letter the pair has taken from the bag. The pair then read the letter out loud.

6. Once each pair has a letter, they have to make up three words with that letter.

7. They then team up with another pair and put their six words together.

8. Next, they try to make a phrase with these words.

9. If there are not enough words to make a phrase, they should go round other pairs to find a word they can swap with them to make their phrase sensible.

Optional Activity

They can do the practical activity by pasting all the words together on a piece of art paper in some sort of order – if there are 30 children in total that would be 15 groups and altogether 45 words.

Red Herring

Bring a game of Scrabble in and have a team Scrabble competition.

Also use the internet for information about board games that help with reading. Try to get at least one of these games and try it out with the children. Then ask them to make up their own game to help with vocabulary and reading.

Websites

Phonetic activity sheets – at www.teacherspayteachers.com

Board games that teach reading and language skills – at http://engagedfamilygaming.com

Board games for reading and spelling – at www.thechaosandtheclutter.com

Dewey Decimal

403

4 All about the Horse

Struggling readers will shy away from reading aloud. Reluctance to read only serves to reinforce a negative view of reading. It is important to reverse this. Shared reading is one way of providing the child with reading practice but in a safe way. This activity is carried out with one other child; if possible, the child with dyslexia should be able to choose his/her shared reading buddy. This can help to take some of the strain and pressure away from the child.

The aim of this activity is therefore to engage in a shared reading session with a friend, to practise reading accuracy, and eventually to explore in depth, looking at the importance of the text. For this activity, we have chosen the horse, and specifically during different historical periods.

Requirements

- the book *War Horse* by Michael Morpurgo
- the DVD of the film *War Horse*

Vocabulary

Verb: gallop

Adjective: blistering

Noun: horse

Associated Words

Word	Meaning and example
reins	
saddle	
transport	
racing	
stirrup	
stable	
annotation	

Main Activity

In order to prompt discussion, have a group reading session using shared reading, or read to the children or ask for volunteers. It is important that this introductory session can provoke some discussion on the book.

It is interesting to look at the evolution of the horse. What can you find out about how the horse evolved? Try to look as far back as 45 million years ago – at that time it was called 'Eohippus'.

Can you try to work out why horses became more 'domestic'? The clue to this relates to transport, farming and industry. Horses in many ways set the path for motor cars – they served a similar purpose for many years prior to the car. It is believed that a fast horse can travel at around 55 miles per hour. It is little wonder that they were used as the 'Pony Express'!

Watch the first 20 minutes of the *War Horse* DVD.

This research will give the children an introduction to the role of the horse in history. Evidence indicates that pre-reading discussion is one of the biggest single indicators of success in reading, so it is important that this stage is not skipped.

The children will then be using shared reading from *War Horse* by Michael Morpurgo. The book can be used simultaneously with the DVD or separately.

Optional Activity

The children can do a warm-up drawing with each hand, to engage both sides of the brain. This can be a drawing of anything at all. Then they can do a drawing of a horse. Next, they can make some annotation notes about the drawing.

Discuss the phrase 'horsing about'. What does this mean? Research it using the library or internet. Discuss the phrase and write some sentences using it. See 'The Origins of 12 Horse-Related Idioms' on mentalfloss.com.

The book *Farewell to the Horse* by Ulrich Raulff gives a history of the horse.

Red Herring

Consider the following points:

- What was happening in the world in 3000 BC? Focus on Egypt and one other part of the world for comparison.

- Can you think of any famous horses? (For example, *Black Beauty* (novel), Napoleon (*Animal Farm*), Trigger (Roy Rogers), Red Rum (horse racing).)

- What sports do horses feature in at the present time? (For example, horse racing, polo, show jumping.)

Tip

The 'hand' is an ancient unit of measurement that is still used for measuring horses. Explore this further and use 'hands' to measure some large objects in the surrounding environment.

Websites

Horse drawing – at www.from-sketch-to-oil-painting.com

Hand (unit of measurement) – at https://en.wikipedia.org

Mitchell and Kenyon film – at www.youtube.com

Dewey Decimal

636

5 Reading for Purpose

We recall asking some eight- and nine-year-old children what the purpose of reading was (Reid 2016), and the majority of the responses centred round the idea of pleasing the teacher or aspects of reading accuracy. Few seemed to relate the purpose of reading to acquiring information.

The aim of this activity is therefore to encourage reading in everyday circumstances, using the language and literacy prompts all around us. Additionally, this activity can also help to develop automaticity and confidence in reading, particularly relating to instructions and general information.

Requirements

- empty Lyle's Golden Syrup 454g tins, thoroughly cleaned, or an alternative product container
- iPad/computer
- A4 question sheet (described below)

Vocabulary

Verb: bake

Adjective: scrumptious

Noun: flapjack

Associated Words

Word	Meaning and example
syrup	
lion	
GDA (Guideline Daily Amount)	
sweetness	
strength	
connotation	

Main Activity

Start by introducing the main aim of the activity, which is to use literacy-rich text which is all around us to help strengthen working knowledge of language and how it is used in a variety of everyday ways.

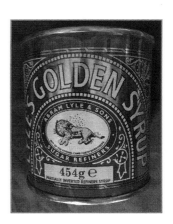

Use the example of reading a Lyle's Golden Syrup tin or similar item of packaging.

Issue one empty, clean tin to each child in the group.

Read the writing on the tin together.

Conduct a discussion on the information on the label of the tin – nutrition information, calories, etc. Then develop a discussion of the text on the tin. You can prompt this discussion by focusing on health, marketing, presentation and purpose.

Next, issue the children with a question sheet containing ten (tin – pun!) questions. One of the questions will be a task to get into the tin which contains a flapjack (made with Lyle's Golden Syrup[1]). Tape a coin to the base of the tin for the children to solve (how to open) and gain access to their flapjack.

Ask the children to make up some questions for their peers from the website – for example, what wars has Lyle's been involved in? You will see that they used a cardboard container at one point – why was this? Children using a PC can then print out questions to exchange with their peers.

Optional Activity

Log in to Lyle's website and make notes about the timeline and history of the company. Print out the copies required.

The image of a dead lion with the quotation provides a good talking point, and can be used for extra research. It was painted by a 19th-century artist who was a favourite of Queen Victoria. The original painting is displayed in Manchester Art Gallery. The quotation has religious connotations and can be used to discuss this topic.

Red Herring

Find out five key facts about lions. Where is their natural habitat? What symbolism is associated with lions? Discuss zoos, and issues surrounding animals in captivity. For basic facts about lions, search the internet.

Discuss the term 'gramme'. What is it, and when was it first used as a measurement?

---

1   You can either ask the children to make flapjacks at home under parental supervision (they may want to team up with other children to do this) or buy them from a supermarket.

Tip

The fun element of this activity is enhanced with the memorable enjoyment of eating a flapjack.

Websites

Lyle's Golden Syrup – at www.lylesgoldensyrup.com

Golden Syrup recipes – at www.lylesgoldensyrup.com

Guideline Daily Amount – at https://en.wikipedia.org

GDA information from a food manufacturer – at www.unilever.com

Dewey Decimal

610

6 Genre

It is important that children with dyslexia are introduced not only to print but also to the world of books. By accessing different types of books they can develop an understanding of 'genre', what that means and how different genres can have an impact on the reader.

The aim of this activity is to help the children gain confidence and working knowledge of genre as a style or category of art, music or literature, and how certain art forms and groups of films can be categorised. This can extend the child with dyslexia in positive terms of his/her thinking about books and reading.

Requirements

- choose a suitable extract from *Northern Lights* for discussion
- computer and access to the internet

Vocabulary

Verb: transform

Adjective: golden

Noun: compass

Associated Words

Word	Meaning and example
category	
class	
group	
bracket	
variety	
type	
style	

Main Activity

Provide examples of different genres (see below) and discuss these.

- science fiction
- drama
- fantasy
- action and adventure
- romance
- mystery
- horror
- satire

The focus will be on fantasy. Watch the trailer for *The Golden Compass* on YouTube.

This film is based on a story by Philip Pullman, *The Golden Compass*, which is also known by the title *Northern Lights*.

You should now discuss the genre of fantasy. You can watch a video about Philip Pullman's book *Northern Lights* on YouTube.

Northern Lights is the first part of Philip Pullman's acclaimed *Dark Materials* trilogy. The book was first published in 1995, a year in which the book also claimed the Carnegie Award.

You can also read reviews of the book, which often draw a comparison with J.K. Rowling's *Harry Potter* series.

Optional Activities

Literature has four main genres: poetry, drama, fiction, non-fiction. Within these, the content can include romance, horror, mystery, comedy, science fiction, action and adventure.

Look at 'Eleanor Rigby' by the Beatles. The genre is classified as rock music.

A music genre is a conventional category that identifies some pieces of music as belonging to a shared tradition or set of conventions. It is to be distinguished from musical form and musical style, although in practice these terms are sometimes used interchangeably. The lyrics in Eleanor Rigby can be classified as poetic.

Look at the YouTube video lyrics of Eleanor Rigby. You will note this is a song about lonely people – and is quite different from many of the romantic songs of the 1960s. If you listen to the background music, you will hear that there are many different types of instruments being used. This also indicates a departure from previous popular music. It can be suggested that the Beatles are experimenting here with genre. This is something, in fact, that the Beatles became quite well known for.

Red Herring

The northern lights can be best seen in Norway. This provides an opportunity to find out key points about Norway, its population and Norwegian history. Travel companies offer holiday breaks to visit the country and see the aurora borealis.

The northern lights can also be seen in the Yukon in Northern Canada. List some advantages of visiting this part of the world. The Travel Yukon website is useful here.

Tip

Print out the lyrics for 'Eleanor Rigby' and ask the children to follow the words while listening to the song. Discuss the meaning of this song.

Websites

Travel Yukon – https://www.travelyukon.com

'Eleanor Rigby' – at www.youtube.com

Northern Lights – at www.visitnorway.com

Dewey Decimal

200, 910

7 Information Leaflet

Opportunities for reading are all around us and it is important that children become aware of that. The message needs to be reinforced that reading is not only about books! Posters, information leaflets, newspapers and advertisements, and even the back of cereal packets – all contain texts that can provide reading practice.

The aim of this activity is to support and enhance field trips through the use of texts and reading material that is found in the everyday environment.

Requirements

- a variety of leaflets promoting attractions and events (examples provided below)

Vocabulary

Verb: imagine

Adjective: informative

Noun: leaflet

Associated Words

Word	Meaning and example
poster	
attraction	
indulge	
pamphlet	

Main Activity

Using a visitor attraction information pamphlet (one per child), examine the content through shared/individual reading and discussion. The following are possible sources of information:

- botanical gardens
- zoological gardens
- waxwork museums
- history museums
- theatre shows
- transport museums (e.g. aircraft, motor vehicles, ships)
- art galleries
- circuses
- time capsules
- landmark structures (e.g. the Falkirk Wheel, Scotland)
- battle sites (e.g. First World War trenches)
- castles
- palaces
- safari parks

Having read the leaflet, either together or individually, ask the children to complete a prepared question worksheet. Ask them to make up some questions themselves – say, five – for their peers. Exchange questions. Follow up with group discussion.

Suggestions for Obtaining Text for Reading

Areas of natural beauty such as beaches, tropical island resorts with coral reefs, and hiking and camping in national parks, mountains and forests – these are examples of traditional tourist attractions to spend summer vacations. Other examples of cultural tourist attractions include historical places, monuments, ancient temples, zoos, aquariums, museums and art galleries, botanical gardens, buildings and structures (e.g. castles, libraries, former prisons, skyscrapers, bridges), theme parks and carnivals, living history museums, ethnic enclave communities, historic trains and cultural events. Factory tours, industrial heritage and creative art and crafts workshops are the object of industrial tourism and creative tourism. Many tourist attractions are also landmarks.

Tourist attractions are also created to capitalise on legends such as a supposed UFO crash site near Roswell, New Mexico, and the alleged Loch Ness monster sightings in Scotland. Ghost sightings also make tourist attractions.

Ethnic communities may become tourist attractions, such as Chinatowns in the United States, and the black British neighbourhood of Brixton in London. In the United States, tourist attractions are advertised on billboards alongside highways and roadways, especially in remote areas. Tourist attractions often provide free promotional brochures and flyers in information centres, fast food restaurants, hotel and motel rooms or lobbies, and rest areas.

Optional Activity

Choose an attraction within of your local area and visit as a follow-up to the activity. Children can carry out project work on the chosen attraction and look up websites to plan their visit.

For a group activity, plan the visit and bear in mind that, depending on the children's ages, they can be involved in organisation (providing a sequential focus to learning). Consider the attraction topic and the time/period in history. This can be linked in with curricular work.

Red Herring

Encourage the children to research and produce their own attraction leaflet. The children can gain information about layout, printing and finishing, and the method(s) of distribution of the leaflets to outlet points from the internet.

Tip

Collect enough free leaflets/pamphlets for all children from distribution outlets such as tourist information centres, libraries, railway stations and airport concourses. There are a large number of attractions in most areas, and many will have a visitor centre with promotional material available. It is a great way to extend knowledge of the locality.

Websites

Tourism leaflets online – www.tourismleafletsonline.com

The power of visitor leaflets and brochures – at http://takeonemedia.co.uk

Tourist attraction – at https://en.wikipedia.org

London, UK – https://www.visitlondon.com

Canada – www.visit-canada.com

Vancouver, Canada – www.tourismvancouver.com

Scotland – https://www.visitscotland.com

USA – www.usatourist.com/english/traveltips/state-tourist-offices.html

Australia – https://www.australia.com/en-us

New Zealand – https://www.newzealand.com/int

Dewey Decimal

900

Spelling

8 Spelling Corks

Children with dyslexia learn more effectively with a task that is active and fun. Games are an excellent way of doing this, particularly with spelling. Spelling can be a considerable hurdle for children with dyslexia – they have difficulty in retaining the sequence of letters in a word and remembering spelling rules. They need a great deal of practice and overlearning. Spelling Corks is geared to overlearning and also the fun element in learning. This activity also focuses on coordination and estimation of distance as it involves dropping and aiming the cork in such a way that it lands on its end, with each letter of a word.

The aim of this activity is to improve spelling and focusing as well as to provide practice in coordination and the estimation of size and distance.

Requirements

- corks
- spelling cards (described below)
- access to a computer and the internet (optional)

Vocabulary

Verbs: spell, drop

Adjectives: tricky, consistent

Noun: cork

Associated Words

Word	Meaning and example
practice	
balance	
land	
turn	
repeat	
complete	

Main Activity

First, you need to practise using a cork on its own. Drop the cork carefully and try to get it to land on its end. You do this by holding the cork horizontally, with thumb and forefinger at each end, and not far above the table surface. Once you have mastered this skill, use it to help with spelling. Once you can successfully land the cork on its end and get three out of three, then you can start the spelling activity.

You will then need to make up a spelling pack. These will be like playing cards, each with one word that the child has difficulty spelling. When printing the word, spread the letters out. For example, if the word to be spelt is 'ball', then write it like this:

B A L L

The child drops the cork on to its end and then says the letter, repeating until the whole word is spelt.

Instructions for Activity

1.   Select a word from the spelling pack to spell.

2.   Say the word.

3.   Spell it aloud three times.

4.   Optional: copy and write the word down.

5.   Turn the word over, or leave it displayed.

6.   Hold the cork horizontally between your thumb and index finger (either hand). The height that the cork should be held is around the length of the cork being used (this also helps with estimation of size and distance).

7.   Drop the cork, trying to make it land upright, on one end.
     When successful, say the first letter of your word.

8.   Continue with the next letter, repeating 'B, B, B' until successful, then 'B A, B A', and so on. Continue until the word is completed.

9.   Then you say your word – BALL.

10. Spell it aloud – B A L L – and write it down: BALL.

Optional Activity

Ask the child to define what a cork is. What are the properties of a cork? Where do corks come from? Look this up in a dictionary or on the internet.

Write down three simple sentences describing cork. This can be a good way to practise using adjectives.

Red Herring

There is a town in the Republic of Ireland called Cork. Find out some facts about Cork. Tourist websites can help.

Select the three best attractions in Cork, and create your own leaflet about Cork.

Tip

When doing the main activity, it is a good idea to start with an easy word, and then progress to more challenging words.

Websites

Cork (city) – at https://en.wikipedia.org

Spelling games – at www.education.com

Dewey Decimal

400, 794, 795

9 Spelling Golf

This can be a popular activity, and it really does help with spelling. It can also help with coordination, which can be a difficulty for children with dyslexia. It is good practice in self-control, as they have to apply pressure in varying amounts when undertaking this activity.

The aim of this activity is to support spelling and also engage with at least two different activities simultaneously, which can help with coordination.

Requirements

- a putting club
- three golf balls
- a cylindrical piece of cardboard or a tin tube
- double-sided tape to fix the cylinder or tube to floor

Vocabulary

Verbs: spell, aim

Adjectives: accurately, skilfully

Nouns: target, putter

Associated Words

Word	Meaning and example
aim	
putter	
grip	
speed	
accuracy	
points	
shot	

Main Activity

Begin this activity with discussion of the vocabulary and associated words shown above.

You need also to select some vocabulary words that can be used as the target word for spelling. Children can choose words for their peers, but initially these should be no longer than 3–4 letters. The words are written on a whiteboard, or on A4 paper, landscape format, and fixed with Blu tack. The children then look at the words displayed.

In turn, they say each word out loud. They then spell the word out loud, repeat the word and use a putter to strike a golf ball gently towards a target (this can be a cylindrical tube lying on its side). After striking the ball, the child spells the word out loud before the ball reaches the target. The harder they strike the ball, the less time they have to spell the word, so encourage speed control.

Begin with shorter words and increase the length. Vary the distance to suit needs and difficulty. Most rooms should be able to accommodate this activity. You can stick the words on walls for display.

Optional Activity

You might want to try this outside – this can be more challenging because of weather conditions and also hard and uneven surfaces. You may also want to video this, so that the children can watch their performance.

Red Herring

Find out about the origins of golf from the internet.

Scotland is well known as the home of golf, because it has some very challenging golf courses. What makes a golf course challenging? Look at some famous golf courses on the internet and suggest why they are challenging for golfers.

Dewey Decimal

400, 794, 795

10 Spelling Ping-Pong

It has already been noted that children with dyslexia can learn more effectively through games and interactive tasks. Spelling Ping-Pong is very interactive as the children work in pairs. Any game that is enjoyable and helps with spelling is of great benefit. This game can also be a form of relaxation and de-stressing the child.

The aim here is to support spelling by making the activity enjoyable. This is also a confidence-building activity.

Requirements

- a table large enough to play table tennis
- two table tennis bats
- some ping-pong balls
- a net (if that is not available, use piles of books instead)

Vocabulary

Verb: serve

Adjective: spinning

Noun: club

Associated Words

Word	Meaning and example
net	
ball	
bat	
score	
table	
tennis	
hit	
gently	
sequence	

Main Activity

First demonstrate this activity with one or two children, and use this as an opportunity to model the rules. Decide yourself what the rules are, but it is helpful to stick to the rules of table tennis.

Write a word on a whiteboard or something similar near the table. Children look at the displayed word – for example, T E N N I S – and/or write out the word themselves to practise spelling the word. They say the word out loud (in turn) and then spell the word out loud (in turn).

The next stage involves two children who face each other with the chosen word – TENNIS – to spell. As child one hits the ball, s/he says the first letter, 'T'. The opponent says 'E' as s/he returns the ball. The children carry on alternating until the word is spelt, or the rally breaks down. Begin by spelling the word once. As the skill develops, the children can carry on repeating the word as long as the rally lasts.

This activity can help with focus and concentration, and can also develop automaticity as the child is carrying out two activities simultaneously – saying the letter and hitting the ball. This is good for auditory–kinaesthetic integration.

Optional Activity

As an optional extension to this, give the child the word to spell just as they start playing the game, so they have not been able to practise. This can be challenging, but also fun.

Red Herring

Look at the history of table tennis on the internet.

Table Tennis and the Cold War

On April 6th, 1971, the US table tennis team was invited on an all-expenses-paid trip to play in China. Four days later, nine players, four officials and two spouses crossed the bridge from Hong Kong to the Chinese mainland. They were the first group of Americans to be allowed into the country since the communist take-over in 1949. One of the first signs during the Cold War of improved relations between the United States and China, *Time* magazine called it 'the pong heard throughout the world. It was shortly followed with a visit to China by President Nixon.

Source: from http://iml.jou.ufl.edu

Read the extract above. What was the Cold War? What does the term 'improved relations' mean?

Dewey Decimal

400, 794, 795

11 Spelling – Be a Teacher

Spelling is a complex skill. It requires a number of sub-skills including phonological awareness, visual memory and knowledge of spelling conventions and rules. These have also to be applied consistently, and in context. In other words, spelling takes place while the child is doing something else – for example, while engaged in a piece of creative writing. This can place spelling secondary, and the result may be an inconsistent and fluctuating pattern to spelling.

The aim of this activity is to help the child develop consistency and accuracy in spelling, and particularly to help children to practise using visual spelling techniques.

Requirements

- a passage for children to correct (example provided below)

Vocabulary

Verb: spell

Adjective: correct

Nouns: paired spelling, homophone

Associated Words

Word	Meaning and example
weather	
forecast	
litter	
climate	
tornado	

Main Activity

Read the passage and correct the spelling. When two different words sound the same but have different meanings, they are called homophones. Sometimes they may also be spelt differently. The passage below has many misspellings, and these include some homophones. You need to correct the misspellings and homophones.

The winde blue very strangely – I had red about it in the newspaper and tooday was the dey. Yesterday it was so fare and very present and the son was shining all dey. Now today the streets were littered with allsorts of thinges and this is set to continue for the rest of the weak. Papers, food scraps, waist and even people's male are all over the plaice. Last knight it was so pieceful – this is certainly a surprise. A whole was opening up on the ground before hour very eyes.

Optional Activity

Make up a chart with visuals showing pictures of the two words that sound the same but have different meanings (homophones). Try to make a visual of each of the words that will help others to guess the meaning of the word.

Red Herring

This activity can provide an excellent lead-in for paired spelling and peer tutoring in spelling. Look at the steps for peer tutoring in spelling on the internet. Get the children to try this out.

There are many variations of paired spelling. Below is one variation.

In paired spelling, two children sit down together and talk through the words they have to learn to spell. Together, they look at the internal structure of the word, and note any patterns, visual clues or mnemonics that will help them remember the spelling.

One child covers the word while the other writes it down. The child checks his or her own spelling to see if it is correct. If so, roles are reversed, and the process continues with the next spelling.

Another example is cued spelling. The steps for this are:

1. Children select a word to learn or are given target words.

2. Pairs enter the words into their spelling diaries.

3. Pairs read the word together.

4. Speller and helper choose cues together.

5. Pairs repeat cues aloud.

6. Speller says cues, while helper writes word.

7. Helper says cues, while speller writes word.

8. Speller writes word quickly and says cues aloud.

9. Speller writes word quickly.

10. Speller reads word aloud.

The technique also includes daily reviews, where the child writes all the words for the day and checks them. The wrong words are then noted and the child goes through the ten steps again for these words. The cued spelling technique is highly interactive and attempts to eliminate the fear of failure through the use of prompt correction procedures.

Website

Confusing words – at www.gingersoftware.com

Dewey Decimal

403

12 Target Words and Visual Connections

There is a strong visual element in spelling. In fact, many words can be spelt and remembered visually. This is important for irregular words that may not follow phonologically regular rules. Practice at using visual techniques for spelling is important. As in many of the other activities in this book, practice and overlearning are key factors.

The aim of this activity is to help to build up the bank of words that children can spell automatically and consistently, and also to help them to use visual imagery and visual skills to aid spelling and build up general visual skills.

Vocabulary

Verb: visualise

Adjective: colourful

Noun: target

Associated Words

Word	Words that symbolise each word
green	
tree	
grass	
peas	

Main Activity

An example of an activity for using visual cues is shown below:

1. Select a target word and six other associated words.

2. The associated words need to have some visual connection to the target word.

3. Give the child the target word and using the 'look, say, cover and write' procedure (see previous activity) ask the child to learn to spell the target word.

4. They then have to:

    -   look at the associated words and discuss how they can be connected visually to the target word (this could be through the meaning of the word, the colour represented by the word or the visual configuration of the word)

    -   spell the associated words and insert them into the table above

    -   learn the word using the 'look, say, cover and write' procedure.

Repeat this at various times over the next few days.
Add a new target word to the list each week, and repeat the above sequence.

Red Herring

Choose a short YouTube clip – an advert would be ideal, because they are usually quick and snappy. Children each choose a target colour, and they only get to view the clip once. They have to write all the items they see that match the target colour. This task can be done in groups of three – two people can be writers, and the other one the caller. This activity has the makings of a group competition.

Red Herring Twist

As an added activity, the caller can get a dictionary and check the spellings of the writers – then all three need to practise any words that were misspelt, and use these as target words for the future.

Websites

Imagery for Kids website – www.imageryforkids.com

How to help children visualise – at www.relaxkids.com

Dewey Decimal

400, 753

13 Syllables, Syllables, Syllables

Knowing and understanding different parts of speech is important for spelling, as the word can be more easily broken down into smaller parts. This can be an aid to remembering spelling rules and spelling conventions. The aim of this activity is to develop an understanding of the division of words, in order to support spelling development.

Requirements

- flashcards (make up appropriate cards)
- a syllable worksheet

Vocabulary

Verb: divide

Adjective: effective

Noun: vowel

Associated Words

Word	Other associated words
syllable	
clap	
method	
realise	
count	

Main Activity

Start with a discussion. What are syllables? Once you have a response to this question, issue flashcards with a definition of syllables. An example is given below.

> A syllable is the sound of a vowel (A, E, I, O, U) that is created when pronouncing the letters A, E, I, O, U or Y.
>
> The letter 'Y' is a vowel only if it creates an E or I sound. For example: silly, funny, happy, easy, fry, try, cry and dry.
>
> The number of times that you hear the sound of a vowel is the number of syllables in a word.

All words have at least one syllable. A syllable is a unit of speech. For example, the word 'yesterday' is broken up into three parts, or syllables – one for each piece of sound you pronounce before you momentarily pause: yes-(pause)-ter-(pause)-day.

Knowing how to divide words into syllables greatly helps with spelling and reading skills, as well as the ability to pronounce words correctly.

This activity will help the children to identify the number of syllables in a word and count the beats in a word; they will understand that one-beat words are shorter than two- and three-beat words.

The following methods can be used.

The 'Chin Method'

1. Place your hand just beneath your chin.

2. Say the word.

3. How many times does your chin touch your hand?

This is the number of syllables.

The 'Clapping Method'

Clapping may help you find syllables.

1. Say the word.

2. Clap each time you hear A, E, I, O or U as a separate sound.

The number of claps is the number of syllables.

Optional Activity

Search the internet for additional tips on spelling. There are also spelling strategies that focus on learning how to use your memory more effectively. Include strategies such as sounding out the word, using memorable details (e.g. 'believe' has a 'lie' in it), and picture words (create pictures from the symbols).

Red Herring

Think of your own Red Herring activity! Or ask the children to make one up.

Dewey Decimal

421

Written Expression

14 Churchill

Winston Churchill is a well-known figure, and many children will be very familiar with him, what he did and what he stood for. Some, however, may not be so familiar. It is a good idea, therefore, to provide an outline introduction of the man – the era he lived in, the importance of that era and why he was an important figure. Use a short video clip of Churchill in action to engage the children's interest. YouTube has a number of famous Churchill speeches.

It is a good idea to provide a schema of Churchill, and the events of the time during which he became famous. Children with dyslexia usually need a schema to assist with memory and organisation. This will also enhance their understanding.

The aim of this activity is to develop written work. This will be much easier with a familiar figure or topic. Although this would be an ideal exercise for the subject of history, it does not need to be confined to that. The aim is not to enhance historical knowledge (although it should help with that), but to assist with expressive writing. This activity can therefore be used any time and it can also be seen as a cross-curricular activity.

Requirements

- short text (provided on the following page)

Vocabulary

Some of the grammar and expressions that stem from Churchill that can be developed and re-enforced are shown below:

Verb: 'doing a Churchill' (showing strength and resoluteness)

Adjective: 'Churchillian' (meaning strong and steadfast)

Noun: Churchill (Winston)

Associated Words

Some of the key words that can be discussed to help the child develop a richer background of the man include the following. It will be useful to copy the chart below, and the child can complete it after the discussion.

Key word	Meaning and example
steadfast	
leader	
inspiration	
defiant	
popular	
stature	
politician	

Main Activity

This activity will also help to develop memory skills, but it will mainly focus on the organisation of written work and the use of headings, sub-headings and bullet points. This can also help the child with note-taking. Many children with dyslexia have difficulty taking appropriate notes, and often tend to copy the information from a book verbatim. The aim of this activity is to avoid that!

The child will need to read the text below. If the child's reading is not at the level of the text, read it to them, or digitally record it and they can play it on their own, and pause and play back as necessary.

Churchill was born in 1874. Although there was a great deal of poverty in England at the time, his family was very wealthy and can be described as aristocratic.

Winston Churchill was born at Blenheim Palace in Oxfordshire. Today, Blenheim Palace is a popular visitor attraction and a World Heritage site.

Churchill was educated at Harrow, one of the top public schools in the country. Usually at that time only aristocrats went to Harrow, but now, although it is still seen as elitist, it attracts high-ranking military personnel and many famous people from all walks of life – for example, James Blunt (singer), Benedict Cumberbatch (actor) and Edward Fox (actor) went to school there. Harrow is also where many top politicians were educated, and Winston Churchill is no exception.

Churchill then went to the Royal Military Academy at Sandhurst. This is also where Prince William and Prince Harry did their military training.

After Sandhurst, Churchill became an officer in the Fourth Hussars, and took part in the Battle of Omdurman in 1898.

Churchill was also an accomplished writer, and during the Boer War (1899–1902) he was a war correspondent. Churchill was actually captured and held prisoner, but he gallantly escaped. Churchill became First Lord of the Admiralty during the First World War (1914–1918), and Prime Minister during World War II (1939–1945).

Ask the children why this piece of text may be difficult to remember. They will likely say that although it is a short piece of text, it contains lots of information, specific names and detail. The aim of this activity is to help the child to arrange and organise the detail for recall and for the development of a piece of written work.

Note: to obtain all the information you need using this framework you may have to read further than the text above, but it is good practice to see how much information you can obtain from this text and how much easier it is to retain and recall the information.

Here are some handy hints for organising the material in preparation for written work and strengthening memory:

1. Think of an appropriate heading for the written work – for example, 'Sir Winston Churchill.' Or encourage them to be creative and think of something unique.

2. Sub-headings are important. For example:

   - Churchill's family

   - Churchill's life

   - Churchill's education

   - Churchill's achievements

3. Bullet points can help the child to identify the key points, and this can be good for practising note-taking. Examples are shown here, but you may want to give the children only one example, and they can do others themselves:

   Churchill's family:

   - Lord Randolph Churchill – father

   - 7th Duke of Marlborough – grandfather

   - Wealthy family

   - Famous family

   Churchill's life:

   - Born – Blenheim Palace in Oxfordshire

   - Officer in Fourth Hussars

   - Took part in the Battle of Omdurman in 1898

- War correspondent during the Boer War

Churchill's education:

- School – Harrow

- Royal Military Academy at Sandhurst

Churchill's achievements:

- Entered prestigious Harrow without completing exam!

- Captured in Boer War and held prisoner

- Took part in the relief of Ladysmith

Optional Activity

Find out more about Churchill – add more sub-headings and bullet points. Watch the most recent movie on Churchill and consider if it is a good representation of him – write down some of Churchill's characteristics based on the movie or your reading. Try to show why you think this.

Red Herring

- World War II warfare – find out the types of weapons used.

- London in wartime – how do you think the people of London felt during the air raids? Google some stories of people during the air raids in London, or near where you live (if applicable).

- Royal Air Force – find out about the different squadrons of the RAF during the war.

- Famous Churchill quotes – this is fun, as there are lots of famous quotes! You may want to perform a play using Churchill quotes.

Tip

It might be a good idea to ask the child to make headings and sub-headings on other topics such as a football match or popular TV programme. This will give them practice at this, and assist a great deal in what is often difficult for children with dyslexia – getting started!

Dewey Decimal

940.53

15 Frame It

It is well established in both research and practice that children with dyslexia need a structure. This is extremely important for written work. Writing frames provide a helpful method of providing that structure. Writing frames can be quite challenging to develop, so it is important that you provide an appropriate structure to help – not just with the development of writing, but also to assist in creativity and getting the child to think laterally and more deeply about the topic.

The aim of this activity is to help the child to develop more sophisticated writing skills, using a wider vocabulary, and also to move away from the obvious to the less obvious and perhaps creative.

Requirements

- writing frames (as described below)

Vocabulary

Verb: argue

Adjective: relevant

Noun: structure

Associated Words

Discuss these words and the parts of grammar they represent with the children. You can also, as seen below, introduce new words that may be relevant to the topic or the development of writing frames. The child can write the meaning and example in the space provided. You may want to copy this table or make up one related to the topic.

Word	Meaning and example
analyse	
discuss	
compare	
dissect	
conclude	
compelling	

Main Activity

1. Provide the children (they can do this in pairs) with an example of a writing frame.

2. For example, you may suggest the following frame for school (it can be adapted for other contents):

Writing Frame

Title: The Arguments for and against Compulsory Litter Collection Duty at School

I think that everyone should be requested to perform litter collection at

school because _____,

but at the same time we have to consider the arguments against this.

For example, some people argue it is more important to educate people

to take more care of litter disposal, and this view is important because

_____.

Considering both those views, I think that _____.

If I were to suggest a slogan (catchy phrase) for keeping the school litter-free,

it would be _____.

Once they have completed this by filling in the blanks, they should make up their own writing frame in groups, and present it to another group and vice versa. They can choose their own topic. Some suggestions are:

- the prefect system
- global warming
- recycling – useful or useless?
- out-of-town malls – what's happening to our town centre?

Red Herring

Think of other meanings of the word 'frame'. Make a list of these – such as picture frame, or being accused of something you did not do.

Find out about the TV programme *You've Been Framed!* by using YouTube. Why is this programme popular? Give your opinions!

Dewey Decimal

807

16 Snippets and More

Many children with dyslexia have difficulty in sequencing. This can be very apparent in written work, when they place information in the wrong part of a story or essay. This difficulty may stem from panic, as they feel they do not have enough information, so just jot down anything that comes to mind. This activity will help them to develop story lines, but also help to sequence information in a coherent and appropriate manner.

The aim of this activity is to help to build up children's vocabulary and their verbal expression, and to sequence and elaborate their writing. It can be a whole-group activity, and it can also be humorous and fun.

Requirements

- the means for some simple note-taking, as described below

Vocabulary

Verb: listen

Adjective: funny

Noun: bystanders

Associated Words

Word	Meaning and example
crowd	
tone	
angry	
unusual	
serious	

Main Activity

Arrange this as a game. Make a list of phrases you may hear when you are passing people on the pavement, or in crowded places such as a café. You would not normally get the full conversation, but only a snippet. The child's task is to use these snippets to make a story.

First, they will need to write down a list of snippets. Examples (these are real snippets!):

- I had no idea.
- That was very strange.
- I could not stop laughing.
- I will not be going there again.
- I am trying to forget this.
- It was the best time I have had for ages.
- I was wishing I were there.

Now the children can write their story using as many of the snippets as they can. It might be a good idea to do this in pairs. We can be relaxed about spelling in this activity. Spelling difficulties can often inhibit children with dyslexia and they may be inclined to restrict their story to the words they can spell. This activity is about creativity, so it is a good idea if spelling is discounted from this one.

Optional Activity

If you want some real snippets, you may get some from:

- a queue of people
- lunch table

- café
- bus
- shopping

Then try to make up another story using another set of snippets.

Red Herring (for More Advanced Children)

Overhearing someone else's conversation is sometimes referred to as 'eavesdropping'. There are articles that say 'Eavesdropping actually makes us better people'. Using the internet for more information, comment on whether you agree with this or not.

Dewey Decimal

807

17 Be a Script Writer

Writing is much more meaningful if it is real and fun, and also if there is a definite purpose to the task. Script writing is a particular kind of writing. The script writer is in control, and writers can take the script in whatever direction they wish. This can allow children with dyslexia to think outside the box, and this can further help with writing. Additionally, script writing mainly uses direct speech. This can be easier for the dyslexic person to write – s/he can write as it sounds in speech! They can even record it orally, and then write it afterwards. It is like having a conversation and developing a story line. This can be a fun activity done in pairs, or even in a small group.

The aim of this activity is to develop vocabulary, imagination and sentence and paragraph writing, and to help the child to enjoy writing.

Requirements

- comics (as many as possible – the child should be able to help with this; it is a good idea if they can use comics they are familiar with as they will already have some form of schema for the text)

Vocabulary

Verb: create

Adjective: fascinating

Noun: script

Associated Words

These need to be added, depending on the story line – the child does this him/herself. After the script has been written, ask the children to note around six key words that can be connected with the story. They can then complete a chart similar to the one below:

Word	Meaning and example

Main Activity

This activity can be carried out in pairs or individually. You will need to obtain some comic strips, photocopy them and then delete the words from the speech bubbles. Children then add words to the comic, based on the pictures. They can think of an appropriate title too. Children with dyslexia often think in pictures, so this type of comic strip may also be used as a framework for other writing projects and activities (such as the one on Churchill in this section). This can be their starting point.

Optional Activity

As a follow-up to this, they can then create their own illustrations and words for a new comic strip. Eventually, they may be able to transfer their completed comic strip into a narrative without pictures, using sentences and paragraphs.

Red Herring

Look at the history of comics on the internet. Search for a decade-by-decade account of the development of comics. Choose one of the decades mentioned, and write a summary of the main comics of that decade – try to work out why these comics were popular.

Dewey Decimal

777

18 Creative Writing Pockets

This activity aims to develop the child's imagination and to translate this into creative writing. It is also a fun activity in the form of a game. Children with dyslexia learn best when they are actively involved in a task, and it is an added bonus if the activity is fun. This activity is both active and fun, and helps to develop word power and imagination.

The aim is to develop creative and imaginative writing through the use of prompts. The prompts are a range of objects that are selected at random. It is important to provide the children with a free choice, as this will help with creativity.

Requirements

- a transparent 'poly pocket'-type bag
- a collection of small objects (put any objects you wish into the bag; try to choose things that can generate discussion)

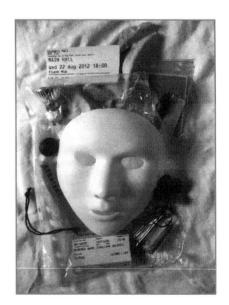

Vocabulary

Verbs: create, invent, produce

Adjectives: scary, amazing, clever

Nouns: magazine, screwdriver, rope

Associated Words

Word	Meaning and example
mask	
ticket	
key	
rag	
map	
wrapper	
bulb	

Main Activity

Ask the children to think about each object. Who might use this object? Where did it come from? The prompts can follow who, where, what, when and how questions. The aim is to get the child to use his/her imagination and inference skills. An example is given below:

Prompt: a door key
How old is the key? What kind of lock/door would it open? Who would own or use this key?

This activity can be handwritten or word-processed. It might be a good idea initially to use chunks of writing and then progress on to linking these using connectives, thereby strengthening sentence structure.

Red Herring

Obtain a mask. The children put on the mask at some point, and this adds to the focus of the activity. For example, ask: How does your appearance change, and how do you feel wearing the mask?

Ask the children to check what they have in their pockets, and get them to create a short story – no more than 100 words – using these prompts. An imaginative story or piece of investigation can follow. For example, Deacon Brodie was an infamous

18th-century Scottish locksmith (key-maker). Look him up on the internet. This can lead into a discussion of the difference between 'infamous' and 'famous'.

Tip

Raiding cupboards and drawers helps to clear out some clutter at home. Make up bags using the items you find.

Websites

40 of the best websites for young writers – at https://study.com

25 helpful websites for creative writers – at https://study.com

Dewey Decimal

Ask the children to find the Dewey Decimal number themselves – but for reference it is 372.6.

19 Rubber Band – A Writing Prompt

Quite often, children with dyslexia can have a vivid imagination and think 'outside the box'. It is important to encourage this, and to use any tool that is available to help with developing their imagination and their writing skills. To develop writing skills, it is important to encourage and develop observational skills and sensory awareness, and therefore to engage in pre-writing preparation. This can involve practice at observing, listening, feeling and using tactile senses. This preparation can form game-type activities – one example, using rubber bands, is highlighted in this activity.

This also helps the dyslexic child to extend their imagination and vocabulary, which is one of the aims of this activity.

Requirements

- rubber bands, preferably large ones, in a variety of colours

Vocabulary

Verbs: stretch, bind

Adjectives: rubbery, brown, strong

Noun: rubber band

Associated Words

Some of the key words that can be discussed to help the child develop their imagination using the properties of a rubber band are shown below. The main points are that the discussion should enrich the child's vocabulary and inspire him/her to develop a richer story.

Key words	Meaning and example
snap	
expand	
ping	
restrict	
hold	

Main Activity

Begin by asking: 'What is a rubber band?' It is a good idea to hand out rubber bands to the children, but first lay down some ground rules! Treat the rubber bands as a friend – with care and no pinging! Ask the children if they can smell a rubber band. Encourage children to use their senses to add their experience to the activity.

In small groups, perhaps of two or three, ask the children to discuss the properties of a rubber band by handling them, using their senses such as touch and smell, and describing the feel of a rubber band. This introductory activity can lay down the foundation for a piece of descriptive writing. Some examples to help the child with the descriptive writing are:

- Write down/describe what a rubber band is.
- Where does a rubber band come from? Use the internet to research this.

They can then move on to a piece of imaginative writing. Write a story that involves a rubber band – perhaps the main character is a rubber band. Give it a name!

Optional Activity

History of Rubber Bands

On March 17, 1845, Stephen Perry of the rubber manufacturing company Messrs Perry and Co, Rubber Co Manufacturing, London patented the first rubber bands made of vulcanized rubber. Perry invented the rubber band to hold papers or envelopes together.

Source: from www.versteegde.nl

Try to find out more about why rubber bands came into widespread use.

Red Herring

As a Red Herring activity children can:

- list five uses for a rubber band

- list five uses for rubber

- think of some pop bands or music albums/CDs that have 'band' or 'rubber' in their title.

Tip

Can you hear a rubber band? Can you smell a rubber band? Encourage the children to use their senses to add experience and understanding to this activity.

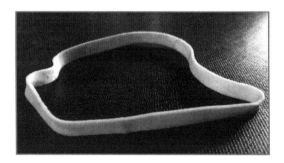

Website

Rubber – at www.explainthatstuff.com

Dewey Decimal

730

20 Bananas

This section focuses on expressive writing, aiming to do this through the child's own experiences. It is a good idea therefore to try to use everyday objects as prompts. This activity focuses on bananas to help develop writing skills.

The aim is develop imagination and writing skills, as well as the child's vocabulary. This activity will also focus on factual writing.

Some words that can be utilised and integrated into the activity – such as smelling, touching, peeling and tasting – can all be discussed with the child, and practical demonstrations can take place. These can all be multi-sensory activities and develop the child's awareness of vocabulary that can be used in descriptive writing.

Requirements

It can be useful to use bananas as a prompt. However, since children will generally be very familiar with this type of fruit, a discussion can take place without any physical materials.

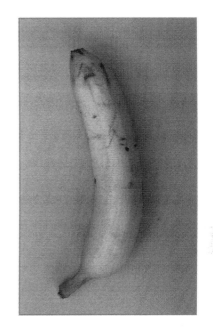

Vocabulary

Verbs: peel, taste

Adjectives: squashy, yellow, appetising

Nouns: banana, bunch

Associated Words

Some of the key words that can be discussed to help children to develop their imagination, using the properties of a banana, are shown below. Discuss these with the children. The discussion should enrich the vocabulary and provide words they can use in descriptive writing.

Key words	Meaning and example
ripe	
fibre	
juicy	

enjoy	
sweet	

Main Activity

Factual Writing

Start with a group discussion: What is a banana? Children can then research this and find out why we eat bananas. How did they come to our country? Look at the history of bananas. Give them a 'heads up' by telling them that bananas are one of the most widely consumed fruits in the world. Eating bananas can help lower blood pressure and reduce the risks of cancer and asthma. Today, bananas are grown in more than 100 countries and are in the top five of the world's food crops in monetary value. Ask the children to find out which country consumes the most bananas in the world.

Definition Task

- Write down/describe what a banana is.
- Describe how you peel a banana.
- List five facts about a banana. Check with a dictionary and on the internet.
- List five ways that bananas can be eaten. With which other foods can they be eaten? Encourage the child to be as imaginative as possible.

Imaginative Writing

Give children a text like the one below as an example, and ask them to try to write an imaginative story about a banana. They could use their own text or they can continue this story.

Title: Bus Banana

I was travelling one morning on a 24 bus to the hospital, catching the bus at 7.50am. As I sat down, upstairs (as it was a double-decker bus), I noticed that there was a banana on its own on the seat opposite mine. It was on the outside seat, and might been left deliberately or by accident. As the bus filled up, the seats were all getting taken and a young woman sat down on the inside seat next to it. A stop later, a young couple got on, and as they approached the seat with the banana, they spoke to the young woman asking about the banana. She replied that it was not hers. There was some chuckling, and the young couple moved to the back of the bus and sat down. I inferred that the young couple and the young woman were medical students and knew each other. My reasoning was that the bus was going to the hospital, where it would terminate, and that most of the passengers – possibly students by their age – would be going there. We reached the hospital and everyone got off the bus; the banana remained seated. The bus service began at 5.00 in the morning, and my journey took about 50 minutes to complete. I wondered how many more journeys the banana would make before someone took pity on it or ate it (is it the same thing?). The banana would have had some tales to tell about the variety of passengers it would have shared many trips with that day. I imagine that the banana would have been eventually removed when the bus returned to the depot for cleaning and preparation for the following day. Inspiration is all around us. This banana certainly captured my imagination!

Source: Nick Guise

Red Herring

Think of your own Red Herring activity! Or ask the children to make one up.

Website

The Banana Police – www.thebananapolice.com

Dewey Decimal

634

21 Tunnock's Teacake

For those who do not know, Tunnock's Teacakes are very much a 'Scottish institution.' They are known and enjoyed all over the world, but if you have not yet had this pleasure, use another similar local delicacy for this activity. The idea behind this activity is to show how a simple everyday article can be used for inspiration and the development of language, ideas and descriptive writing.

The aim is to facilitate descriptive writing through a multi-sensory activity and experience that can also prompt discussion. An additional aim is to improve simple sentence structure and to introduce connectives for linking sentences.

Requirements

- some Tunnock's Teacakes or a local equivalent cake with attractive packaging (it would be good to have a large supply of these, but we are only interested in the foil wrap – we are assuming the contents will have disappeared, or soon will, after the activity!)
- glue
- a glue brush
- containers for glue
- protective cover for the worktop

Vocabulary

Verbs: unwrap, bite, discuss

Adjectives: heavenly, wonderful, awesome

Nouns: foil, cake, shop

Associated Words

Word	Meaning and example
delicious	
chocolate	
bite	
sweet	
aftertaste	
impression	
anticipate	

Main Activity

Issue teacakes to all children, and discuss: 'What is a Tunnock's Teacake?' Read the description of the teacake on the packaging, and then discuss with the group what you experience when eating a cake like this. It is important that you write a description of what the cake is. Imagine you are composing an advert for it. What adjectives would you use?

Make this a multi-sensory task. Describe the complete experience from being given a teacake right through until the last bite and lingering aftertaste. This should lead into descriptive writing.

Optional Activity

Make up an advert for the teacake. Use a full-size blank sheet of paper, and be sure to list its properties and key points and why you should buy one!

Red Herring

List five facts about a Tunnock's Teacake – Google this and look at its origins and history. Find out where they are made. Why do you think this location was chosen?

Another Red Herring

Use the foil wrappers to cover various objects such as a ball, a mask, an old trainer, a shoe box or a hat/cap – make a montage of wrappers. This activity can help with motor skills, as well as develop creativity. See the photo below of examples of things decorated in Tunnock's wrappers.

Tip

Have a box of teacakes or other edible foodstuffs handy at all times; this provides some scope for a discussion of healthy eating and diet, and is great for an instant lesson.

Website

Tunnock's website – www.tunnock.co.uk

Dewey Decimal

641.86

22 VCOP (Vocabulary, Connectives, Openers, Punctuation)

Confidence, or lack of it, can play a big part in the quality and quantity of children's written work. They may have lots of ideas, but lack the confidence to put these down on paper. They may feel that they don't have the vocabulary and that their punctuation is weak.

The aim of this activity is to help children develop confidence in creative and overall writing skills. There are four key areas that can help with this – vocabulary, connectives, openers and punctuation (VCOP), and this is the main theme of this activity.

(Ros Wilson is credited with the development of VCOPs as part of her 'Big Writing' approach to teaching – see the Websites section below. Many free downloadable resources are available.)

Requirements

- spinner wheels
- 'powerful word' sheets (described below)
- literacy resource card (see website provided below)

Vocabulary

Verb: verbalise

Adjective: powerful

Noun: full stop

Associated Words

Word	Meaning and example
vocabulary	
connective	
opener	

punctuation	
structure	
visualise	

Main Activity

This approach focuses on the four core targets – vocabulary, connectives, openers and punctuation (VCOP) – as a way of helping children to improve the structure of their writing. Use the VCOP literacy resource card to assist with developing writing skills and strengths.

An easy-to-use literacy resource card can be downloaded. This card focuses on a number of basic rules – such as how to distinguish between 'of' and 'off', 'there', 'they're' and 'their', etc.

Children find these really useful to have available when they are peer-marking and self-assessing their work, to ensure they are using the rules they have been taught.

Print out copies of the literacy resource card and, if possible, laminate. Encourage children to keep this A4 card with them and use regularly to support their creative writing and grammatical development.

Red Herring

Discuss 'WOW' words – words that use powerful language – with the children – for example: 'dazzling', 'spectacular', 'lively', 'tremendous', 'memorable', 'superb', 'incredible', 'magnificent', 'fascinating', 'exceptional'.

- Taking turns, verbalise a sentence – for example, 'Daisy was wearing a dazzling dress for the end-of-term dance' (alliteration). Begin with simple sentences.

- Make up or use resource word cards for a game of 'Snap'. These can be laminated. Children should verbalise the meaning, using a sentence, when they get a snap.

- Use a spinner wheel to help to recall meanings. Make up word wheels with a variety of key words and interest words (these can be integrated).

- Make up some nine-letter word wheels for use with spinner wheels (see the 'Spinneracy' activity in Section 11). Make up as many two-letter and longer words including the full nine-letter word for children to work on.

Tip

On the TES website, there are many free downloads, with a huge range of VCOP activities.

Websites

Literary Resource Card – at www.tes.com

Big Writing (Ros Wilson) – at https://en.wikipedia.org

VCOP – at www.tes.com

VCOP visuals, ideas and resources – at www.pinterest.com

Dewey Decimal

400

23 Local Language

Children with dyslexia need cues to help with expressive writing. The most effective cues are those that are meaningful to the writer. This activity uses local information and local language.

The aim is for children to find pictures or texts in the environment, which they can use for discussion. These can also be used as prompts for creative and/or factual writing.

Requirements

- a clip board
- a smart phone
- sample imaged texts for modelling/displaying

Vocabulary

Verb: discover

Adjective: clever

Noun: advertisement

Associated Words

Key words	Meaning and example
display	
quotation	
locality	
feelings	
intangible	

Main Activity

Introduce the topic of looking for and noting pieces of text that can be found on our doorstep. Be alert to the richness and creativity of words used for different effects – for example, instructional, informative, influential, supportive, interesting and humorous. Local texts in the environment convey a variety of messages, and can be found in cafés, restaurants, hotels, cinemas and theatres, among other places. A lot of these are inspirational and positive. Although simple, these resources are really helpful for assisting children in sentence structure and imagination.

Discuss the content and the meaning of messages with children. How can they relate to this? The text below uses the three-point approach for effect. This text was displayed on a café wall in Wells, England, and is an example of how text can be used for discussion prompts and meaning.

Optional Activity

Take children outside for a text-gathering exercise. Smartphones are ideal for this, although a clipboard or small notepad, encouraging the writing down of the texts, will be fine. Focus on shop fronts, signage and promotional wording, and posters advertising events. Look for displays on the sides and backs of cars/vans/buses/lorries, where you will see a variety of slogans, advertising and contact details. Street signs for safety and instruction are all around. Spend about half an hour carrying out this research, and bring the results back inside for extension work and discussion. Make up folders for displaying on a smartboard if possible.

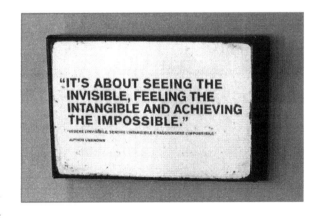

Red Herring

Poetry and lyrics can be prompted and inspired by the texts gathered. There is always the chance that pieces of conversations can be heard, and they too can be incorporated into the writing. Conversations that take place while children purchase items from shops (build in a treat during the visit) can be a rich resource for including in this work. Going round a store is also a good life-skill exercise for looking and seeing where and how goods are located, grouped, displayed and marketed. Text is everywhere!

Tip

Always be on the lookout for amazing language.

Dewey Decimal

400

24 Forest Walk

Learning is more effective if it is meaningful and relates to a naturalistic setting. As children become aware of our environment their vocabulary can be enriched. It is important to capitalise on this, and to use the natural environment as much as possible to develop their vocabulary and comprehension. There are probably quite a number of words related to, for example, a play area that children do not readily use but it could be helpful if they knew. This can apply to almost any aspect of their immediate environment.

The focus of this particular activity is a forest walk. This may be convenient in some cases but less convenient for others – in the latter, it can be incorporated into an excursion.

The aim of this activity is to develop vocabulary and awareness of the environment. This should be seen as a means of developing vocabulary. A forest walk is a good one to start with as there are many facets to a forest, some of which may be familiar to the child. But the idea is to enrich this and help the child accumulate more vocabulary that they can access. This is one of the issues with children with dyslexia. They may know the meaning of a lot of words but have difficulty in accessing these in written work and sometimes orally too. The idea therefore is not just to enrich vocabulary, but to provide a meaningful context for this – a forest walk. This can give them a schema or framework of what is found in a forest and they can access this more readily in written work. It is important to follow up this activity with a written exercise such as 'Life in the Forest.'

Requirements

- maps (one for each group; optional)
- a compass (one for each group; optional)

Vocabulary

Verb: amble

Adjective: green

Noun: birch tree

Associated Words

A number of associated words can be used here. It is important that the child is able to put an example of the word next to it to show they know the meaning of the word:

Word	Meaning and example
snail	
squirrel	
rustle	
deep	
branch	
perimeter	

Main Activity

This can be done as a field trip, or using the internet for information or an internet game. Each group of around three children has to go on a forest walk. This involves:

- the group deciding and planning a route (adult supervision would be required here)
- mapping the route
- deciding what they need to take with them
- writing a journal of the walk
- indicating the different trees, bugs, animals and anything else they might come across.

Children might need some help in using maps and compasses if these are used. This can introduce a cross-curricular perspective – for example, for the subjects of geography, environmental studies or biology.

Optional Activity

Children can try to write an adventure story connected to the walk – give them some possible titles or get the group as a whole to suggest titles.

Red Herring

Find out about rainforests. What are they, and where do you find them? Wikipedia is a good place to start.

Dewey Decimal

400, 508, 577

Vocabulary

25 'A' is for...

Automaticity is an important aspect in reading, and indeed in undertaking most activities. In order to be able to carry out an activity consistently, one needs to acquire a degree of automaticity. The key to acquiring automaticity is practice, and particularly practice at speed. One of the factors that needs to be incorporated into a programme for children with dyslexia is overlearning. That does not mean rote repetition, but practice at acquiring the skill (here it is letter naming) in a number of different contexts. Games, and in particular fun games, are good for this.

The aim of this activity is to help to build up children's vocabulary through overlearning.

Requirements

- paper
- timer
- Blu tack to put children's answers on the wall

Vocabulary

Verbs: scan, observe, search

Adjective: creative

Noun: alphabet

Associated Words

Add some others yourself, depending on the objects you have selected for the wall:

Word	Meaning and example
display	
folder	
text	
presentation	
quantity	
accuracy	

Main Activity

Ensure that there are objects around beginning with each letter of the alphabet. The children work in pairs and are timed and asked to write down objects around them, each one beginning with a different letter of the alphabet. The suggested time is five minutes (depending on the age of the children). Each pair then has to count how many they have found. Then they make up a display alphabet sheet with A to Z and write each object and illustrate it as well as they can – perhaps producing a drawing for each object. When this is completed, each sheet is collected and pinned on the wall without the children's names being displayed. The group then judges the best ones using the following criteria:

- quantity
- presentation
- accuracy.

Optional Activity

Try different versions of this task. For example, ask them to write the names of objects which end with each letter of the alphabet – A = banana.

Red Herring

Ask the children to write an A–Z poem or story with each letter symbolising an event or object.

You can also use an existing well-known structure for a poem such as 'The Minister's Cat is an angry cat and his name is…Alfredo'. Here the children have to think of an adjective and name beginning with each letter of the alphabet (see Wikipedia for more information).

Dewey Decimal

400

26 Poetry Path

It is important to try to develop the vocabulary of children with dyslexia, and to encourage them to use words in as many different ways as possible. Poetry lends itself to this, and also to creativity.

The aim of this activity is to encourage children to create a written, poetic and/or lyrical piece of work. They use the environment as a means of inspiration, and this gives them the opportunity to focus on their senses and to use them to help in the development of a poem.

Requirements

- a clipboard
- a mobile phone/iPad or similar
- a poly pocket transparent bag
- glue

Vocabulary

Verb: stroll

Adjective: rustling

Noun: path

Associated Words

Word	Meaning and example
traffic	
sound	
aroma	
bird	
tree	
colour	
locality	

Main Activity

As an option, prior to beginning this activity, use previous poems and texts that have been produced by other children. However, the activity can progress well with no prompting at all.

The source for this activity can be any local path or track. Where possible, try to use a location that is rich in sensory stimulus. Vary the length to suit availability. Collecting as many images, sounds, smells and ideas as possible along the route enables children to have a wide variety of triggers. Encourage children to gather as much information as possible. Note down anything that can add to the poem or written piece of work when back inside. Children can use mobile devices to capture thoughts and images, and to make notes/sketches. Using a recorder is also useful to support memory and recreate ideas. Using a poly pocket, children can gather scraps of rubbish, leaves, feathers – anything that may help towards their texts. Vary the time of year when doing this activity; this can support seasonal topic work. Optionally, children can collaborate and produce combined texts. There is scope here for rhythm and lyrics for musical development.

Upon completion of the route/path and when back inside, fully discuss the experience and share the vocabulary gathered. Images and any objects can also be discussed and shared. If children have difficulty starting, model four lines of poetry, rhyming or otherwise.

Optional Activity

Children can exchange their word capture with each other, and create a story or poem. For this exercise, limit them to 50–60 words. Being restricted to a maximum word count, this exercise can help the children who struggle with extended writing. Using all the gathered wrappers, leaves, feathers, twigs, etc., the group can create a combined visual display, perhaps making a large graphic montage question mark.

Red Herring

Discuss the famous distance race of 100 yards or 100 metres. What is the difference between metres and yards?

Tip

Encourage children to keep a notebook/diary and to add any interesting words/images that they come across during the week. Encourage looking up – most of the time we tend to look around on a limited lower level, and looking up provides more sources of inspiration. Using a mobile device for image/audio capture allows for a great stream of resourcing and assists memory; it is also great for revision support and overlearning.

Websites

The 100-yard dash – at https://en.wikipedia.org

Speed conversion tool – at www.convert-me.com

Dewey Decimal

530.8

27 Word Wheel

Every opportunity should be taken to develop the child's vocabulary. It does not need to be a vocabulary lesson, but can be a game, activity or even a quiz. The more words the child is exposed to, the better.

The aim of this activity is for the children to have fun with words, using a multi-sensory device. The activity can also assist with spelling and overall word knowledge. Children with dyslexia need overlearning in order to achieve automaticity. This activity is a good source of overlearning.

Requirements

- word wheel puzzle(s) (described below – make up wheels to suit whatever topic the child is doing when learning)

- clear spinner (see website provided below)

Vocabulary

Verb: spin

Adjective: clever

Noun: clue

Associated Words

Word	Meaning and example
wheel	
puzzle	

diagram	
image	

Main Activity

Word wheel puzzles are fun to do, and can be used as a warm-up exercise, a time-filler, a group competitive activity, or a race against the clock! All word wheels work the same way. The aim is to make as many words as you can of two letters or more from the nine letters in the wheel, using each letter in each word only once, and always using the letter in the centre of the wheel. Each wheel will also contain one word which uses up all the letters.

Optional Activity

Create an image wheel using pictures and graphics. This can be made using magazines, scissors and glue. As an option, children can create a wheel using a graphic program if available. Using the spinner wheel, the challenge is to fully describe the image.

Red Herring

Use a spinner wheel to select a beginning letter and word – for example, M and many.

Discuss what 'many' means – verbalise a few examples. Age-appropriate words should be suggested – M and matriculate. This can be extended to sentence development: 'How *many* times did it take James to catch the ball with his other hand?' 'Jane was hoping to *matriculate* in the summer.'

Tip

Make up wheels to suit different topics, and use for fun revision. Work with others to cover the whole of the curriculum. Various websites provide a huge range of suggestions and ideas on how to use word wheels, also offering free word lists, with solutions. Word wheels can also be played online. This complements the tactile method, and enables the child to access this learning tool wherever they are.

Websites

Word wheels – at www.activityvillage.co.uk and www.lovattspuzzles.com

Word wheel game – at www.wordwheels.co.uk

Clear spinners – at www.crossboweducation.com

Dewey Decimal

400, 403

28 Nouns – Flashcards

Learning and using appropriate punctuation can be quite challenging for children with dyslexia. This applies particularly to nouns and the different types of nouns and how to use these. Although children with dyslexia may know that capitals are used for proper nouns, they may not always use them in practice.

The aim of this activity is to help the child become familiar with nouns, and to provide an understanding that a noun is a part of speech that denotes a person, animal, place, thing or idea. This activity can therefore help with the consolidation of noun understanding, through the naming of objects and items. In this way, with practice, children can develop their knowledge of what a noun is. Additionally, the understanding of 'proper' nouns can be reinforced.

Requirements

- blank flashcards of different sizes (small and large)

Vocabulary

Verb: name

Adjective: large

Noun: flashcard

Associated Words

Word	Meaning and example
guess	
describe	
adjective	
alight	

Main Activity

Model a demonstration flashcard with the child – for example, apple – and provide relevant clues such as:

- They come in different colours.

- They are round.

- You will find them in supermarkets.

- They have a core.

- An _____ a day keeps the doctor away.

The children should make up three to four different noun cards with the noun one side and clues on the reverse. In turn, the children verbalise their noun clues until someone guesses correctly.

Example: Bicycle

- It is made of metal and rubber.

- Can be used for fun, work and sport.

- It can go fast or slow.

- You sit on it.

- It has handlebars.

Example: Where am I? (Train Carriage)

- 'Mind the gap.'

- 'Doors closing.'

- 'Tickets, please.'

- Keep on track.

- 'Take care when alighting.' (What does alighting mean? Discuss.)

Optional Activity

Using the nouns, the children can create starters for fiction and/or non-fiction pieces of writing. Using a 50-word maximum guide, children can strengthen their short textual work and can also use the questions as a resource. You can also focus on what a proper noun is.

Red Herring

Pictionary is a great game to complement this activity.

Tip

Advise the children to cover the noun card with their hand while reading out their clues, as their word may be visible on the reverse.

Websites

Nouns – at www.gingersoftware.com

What is a noun? – at www.english-grammar-revolution.com

Dewey Decimal

426, 428

29 Taste Texts

Children with dyslexia often have difficulty with technical and specialised words, and this can apply to food and the food industry in particular. Additionally, it is important that they are able to use words flexibly and effectively. This can help to develop their vocabulary and also help with written work and descriptive writing.

The aim of this activity is to help children to understand promotional words in the context of the food industry. They can also learn how emotive language is used to target consumers. This gives them a fuller realisation of how words can be used effectively.

Requirements

- copies of texts for shared reading (you could use sample texts from restaurants/cafés; an example is provided below)

Vocabulary

Verb: taste

Adjective: spicy

Noun: eggs

Associated Words

Word	Meaning and example
scratch	
seasonal	
shortcut	
tasting	
subliminal	

Main Activity

A sample text should be discussed. For example:

> At EAT, we cook great tasting, seasonal food. We don't believe in taking shortcuts. We cook our food from scratch each day in our kitchen and change our menu with each season. We love making food which puts a smile on your face.
>
> That's why we are on a mission to serve up great tasting, seasonal food every single day.
>
> Source: EAT packaging

Children should discuss how effective the text is, and then try to make up their own text based on their own restaurant/café – they need to think of a name and a text to correspond to that.

Optional Activity

Watch YouTube clips of Jamie Oliver's '5 Things to do with...Chicken!'

> Chicken is one of the most versatile and delicious meats on this planet!
>
> So, here are five of our favourite chicken recipes for you to try at home. These recipes are sure to have your friends and family flocking to yours for dinner!
>
> Source: Jamie Oliver (from www.jamieoliver.com)

Focus on presentation and language. The sequence is important in following a recipe. Ask the children to choose a recipe and break it down into a sequence using numbers.

Red Herring

Discuss and debate health issues and responsibilities associated with the food industry. One of the main areas where fast food companies face regulation is the advertising of 'junk food' to children. In the UK, the Children's Food Bill is intended to highly regulate the advertising of such food aimed at children.

You can also discuss allergies. What are allergies?

Tip

Provide some items of food – healthy and not so healthy – for tasting and discuss the product description (checking with children beforehand for any allergies they may have).

Websites

Fast food advertising – at https://en.wikipedia.org

Jamie Oliver: How to cook roast chicken – at www.youtube.com

Dewey Decimal

394.1

30 Keys

One of the points that need to be highlighted in relation to dyslexia intervention is 'overlearning'! We often hear teachers and parents saying, 'We have shown them how to do this task on countless occasions, and they still make the same mistakes.' This is because in order to achieve automaticity children with dyslexia need overlearning, so one expects to have to repeat things a number of times. This form of repetition can last years – there is no time estimation on how long a dyslexic person needs to achieve automaticity – so it is a good idea to build in overlearning with all tasks.

The aim of this activity is that through repetition and the use of verbs, adjectives and nouns (VAN) in all activities, the children's knowledge and ability will be reinforced and they will achieve automaticity in using grammar effectively.

Requirements

- a variety of old, obsolete keys

Vocabulary

Verb: open

Adjective: skilful

Noun: key

Associated Words

Word	Meaning and example
lock	
unique	
musical	
management	
topic	
torque	
recruited	

Main Activity

Start by asking the children to define what is meant by the word 'key' – they can use online dictionaries – and ask them to compare different definitions of the word 'key':

1. Introduce the word 'key' and ask the children to write down what the word means to them.

2. The children then read the text either individually or in groups.

3. Build up a description of keys. Show children samples of keys and also different types of key for different purposes.

4. Ask the children to suggest what things the keys would open – doors, safes, boxes, lockers, cars (electronic), padlocks, jails (see Deacon Brodie text below).

Optional Activity

Deacon Brodie (William Brodie, 1741–1788)

Deacon Brodie was a well-respected member of Edinburgh society. He was an expert cabinet-maker and a member of the Town Council as well as Deacon (head) of the Incorporation of Wrights and Masons.

Ask the children to produce some text – either handwritten or typed – about Deacon Brodie. Ask them to find out what happened to him – what was his secret? Who are Jekyll and Hyde? Searching the internet should help.

Red Herring

Give children a list of things to find out. For example:

- different uses of the word 'key'
- key types
- key management
- musical key
- key lock
- key player (e.g. in football, rugby, cricket, hockey)
- key worker
- keyboard

It is said that Brodie's bizarre double life inspired Robert Louis Stevenson, whose father had had furniture made by Brodie. Stevenson included aspects of Brodie's life and character in his story of a split personality, *The Strange Case of Dr. Jekyll and Mr. Hyde.*

Source: from www.historic-uk.com

Tip

Nearly everyone has keys that are no longer in use. This is a great chance to get these out of the house and use them for creative stimulus.

Websites

Key (lock) – at https://en.wikipedia.org

Deacon Brodie – at www.historic-uk.com

Ther real Jekyll and Hyde? – at www.bbc.co.uk

Dewey Decimal

600, 620

31 Tongue Twisters

Any activity that manipulates words can be useful for the child with dyslexia. The aim of this activity is that, through the use of tongue twisters, children will have more confidence to use words and differentiate between words that sound similar. This activity can also help with concentration and articulation. Due to the nature and wording of these tongue twisters, children can enjoy the fun element, and this can help them to engage more fully with the task.

Requirements

- lists of tongue twisters for practice

Vocabulary

Verb: twist

Adjective: rapid

Noun: tongue

Associated Words

Word	Meaning and example
articulation	
sequence	
pronunciation	
alliteration	
concentration	
amusement	

Main Activity

A tongue twister is a specific sequence of words whose rapid, repeated pronunciation is difficult, even for native speakers. Often, there are similar words that follow one another, but which differ in certain syllables. Alliterations are also frequent. In addition, some tongue twisters are difficult because of their unusual word composition (sentence structure) and therefore require a high level of concentration. Some tongue twisters are made for amusement; however, professional speakers such as actors, politicians and television/radio hosts use them as articulation exercises.

Children can take turns in reading out loud the following tongue twisters. This activity is fun, and children generally are happy to participate. Speed increase adds to the amusement and is good for focus.

Tongue Twisters

Peter Piper picked a peck of pickled peppers.
A peck of pickled peppers Peter Piper picked.
If Peter Piper picked a peck of pickled peppers,
Where's the peck of pickled peppers Peter Piper picked?

How much wood would a woodchuck chuck if a wood chuck could chuck wood?
He would chuck, he would, as much as he could,
and chuck as much wood as a woodchuck would if a woodchuck could chuck wood.

She sells sea shells by the seashore.

Betty bought a bit of butter.
But the butter Betty bought was bitter.
So, Betty bought a better butter, and it was better than the butter Betty bought before.

Denise sees the fleece,
Denise sees the fleas.
At least Denise could sneeze

How much ground would a groundhog hog, if a groundhog could hog ground?
A groundhog would hog all the ground he could hog, if a groundhog could hog ground.

Irish wristwatch.

Optional Activity

Children can try to make up their own tongue twisters.

Red Herring

The game Twister can be played, if age-appropriate.

It is a game of physical skill, played on a large plastic mat that is spread on the floor. The mat has six rows of coloured circles with a different colour for each row.

Playing Twister can help with concentration and coordination, and is good fun, too.

Tip

Encourage children to practise slowly and build up speed.

Websites

Tongue twisters – at www.smart-words.org

Twister (game) – at https://en.wikipedia.org

Dewey Decimal

790

Part 2

Learning

Introduction

Often the most effective way to develop the learning skills of children with dyslexia is to look at the key factors for effective learning for *all* children. The best practices for children with dyslexia are often best practice for all. The difference is that children with dyslexia may need more reinforcement, the materials may need to be presented in a different way, and a number of considerations have to be kept in mind when developing materials. These can include understanding, planning, action and interaction, and transfer of learning:

1. **Understanding.** The child needs be able to understand the requirements of the task. New learning may need to be repeated or demonstrated.

2. **Planning.** The child needs to be able to identify the key points, and be able to work out a learning plan. For that reason, we have suggested that many of the activities can be carried out in groups.

3. **Action and interaction.** The child with dyslexia will respond more effectively if the task involves action – active learning and also interaction – together with group work and discussion. These factors feature in most of the activities in this book.

4. **Transfer of learning.** Previous learning should help to provide a plan and strategies for tackling new tasks. This is a central aim of this book, and we have built in cumulative learning such as vocabulary and the Dewey Decimal system.

We have also made this part of the book quite broad, including areas such as general knowledge and general science. Children with dyslexia often have a thirst for knowledge and obtain great satisfaction from acquiring information and responding correctly to questions. The problem is that they may have difficulty retaining the information or acquiring the information through reading.

We have used everyday objects, as familiar items can be more within the child's comfort zone and existing schema. Activities relating to pirates, UFOs, trees, water and circuses are found in this part of the book.

We are very aware of the memory issues experienced by children with dyslexia, and have incorporated a range of memory activities and strategies into this part of the book. Once again information can be retained more readily if the context is familiar to the child. Game activities are the most successful way of achieving this. Games also give some responsibility to the child, and this ownership is also important for engaging the child and for successful outcomes. Memory in fact comes into most activities – for example, in the section on learning games for fun, memory would be prominent in the 'We've Got Talent' activity, as they would need to remember the words of a song or details of an act.

The child needs to understand the nature of the task. Comprehension is important, and often children with dyslexia can have good comprehension but may not be able to realise that without sufficient cues and supports. The section on comprehension gets the child to think and comprehend, and also stretches their comprehension to a higher level. There is an activity on critical thinking, and this is very important for children with dyslexia as they are often so preoccupied with reading accuracy that the higher-order meaning of the text is lost.

It is important to appreciate that learning takes place over time. This means that follow-up activities are important, as children can carry these out later and the context will be more familiar as they will not be starting from scratch.

Learning also requires a period of consolidation, and this is important for children with dyslexia. Overlearning is necessary. Often, children with dyslexia may appear to have learned something new – but they may not have consolidated that new piece of learning. They therefore require a period of overlearning in order to ensure they have automaticity in the use of that new learning.

It is important to consider the emotional and social needs of children with dyslexia. This is integral in each of the activities. The nature of the activities promotes team building, and because they are accessible for children with dyslexia, they can promote success and therefore boost self-esteem. Low self-esteem can be at the root of many of the difficulties experienced by children with dyslexia, and we are certain that they will feel better about themselves once they have completed the activities in this part, particularly the section on learning games for fun.

General Knowledge

32 Pirates

We often find that children with dyslexia can score low in general knowledge, although this is not always the case. This is likely because they may not read a lot, or their memory may fail them in terms of retrieving information when asked a general knowledge question. They may need cues and prompts to retrieve the required information.

The aim of this activity is to develop general knowledge, historical knowledge and general awareness of life on the open seas by using 'Pirates' as a topic. The activity also focuses on the dangers experienced by pirates. It also develops reading fluency and constructive questioning, as well as comprehension.

Requirements

The following relate to one of the optional activities (making a pirate map):

- paper (parchment paper is preferred, if available)
- tea for 'ageing' the paper
- a candle for burning the edges of the paper
- sponges

Vocabulary

Verb: threaten

Adjective: famous

Noun: pirates

Associated Words

Word	Meaning and example
treasure	
gold	
swashbuckling	
buccaneer	
plank	

eye patch	
piracy	
combating	

Main Activity

Start with the following reading comprehension text (for group or individual reading):

> The earliest documented instances of piracy are the exploits of the Sea Peoples who threatened the ships sailing in the Aegean and Mediterranean waters in the 14th century BC. In classical antiquity, the Phoenicians, Illyrians and Tyrrhenians were known as pirates.
>
> Source: from https://en.wikipedia.org

When Were Pirates First Recorded in History?

The era of piracy in the Caribbean began in the 1500s, and died out in the 1830s after the navies of the nations of Western Europe and North America with colonies in the Caribbean began to combat pirates. The period during which pirates were most successful was from the 1660s to 1730s.

Eye Patches

It is a pretty common misconception that pirates' eye patches were worn to conceal an empty eye socket. The real reason is much more interesting. Eye patches were worn so that one eye would remain constantly adjusted to darkness, which made it easier to fight below deck when boarding ships. The technique was so effective that keeping one eye closed is still a technique used in the military today for night-time survival.

In small groups, ask the children to devise ten questions about pirates, which they can present to another group.

Who Was the Greatest Pirate of All Time?

The Barbarossa Brothers sailed from North Africa's Barbary Coast. Barbarossa means 'red beard' in Italian. The brothers, Aruj and Hizir, became rich by capturing European vessels in the Mediterranean Sea.

You might find this surprising, but Sir Francis Drake (see Red Herring below) was considered a pirate before becoming a hero.

Other famous pirates were:

- L'Olonnais

- Henry Morgan

- Captain Kidd

- Blackbeard

- Calico Jack

- Madame Cheng.

Find out one fact about each of the above famous pirates. For one of them, use the Dewey Decimal system, if available, in the library.

Optional Activity

Make a pirate map:

1. Take a piece of white paper and tear off all the edges (don't use scissors!).

2. Crumple the paper up as tightly as you can.

3. Flatten the paper out again and put on to a plate or baking sheet.

4. Pour coffee or tea over the paper.

5. Once dry, burn the edges, *if this can be done safely* (remember smoke/fire alarms, etc.).

Another optional activity can be a project on pirates from earliest times to the present day. The internet has a great collection of pirate facts: who they were, what they did, where they did it, and how.

Red Herring

Find out about Francis Drake and the Spanish Armada during the reign of Elizabeth I of England.

How did the traditional sweet 'Tobermory Tattie' get its name? Investigate the 'penny tray' (or equivalent) of inexpensive sweets in the 1960s.

Tip

Soak an A3 piece of paper in cold tea and, once dry, slightly burn the edges with a candle or lighter for the map (optional). The film *Pirates of the Caribbean* can be used as an introductory resource, for fun and/or for film study techniques and language.

Websites

Piracy – at https://en.wikipedia.org

Pirate facts – at www.history-for-kids.com

Treasure map – at www.dltk-kids.com

Dewey Decimal

364.1

33 UFOs (Unidentified Flying Objects)

Space and the universe almost always fascinate children. This is the focus of this activity – to engage children in the topic and to develop their general awareness and knowledge of the universe.

The activity aims to help the children discuss whether there really is intelligent life out there, and where it is. With the solar system seemingly too hot or too cold, or proven to have no life of any type, the hope appears to be in other parts of the universe. The fascinating point about this topic is that there are no definitive answers, and children are at liberty to voice their own opinions.

Requirements

- a reading passage (one is provided below)
- access to a computer and the internet (optional, with supervision)

Vocabulary

Verb: flying

Adjective: saucer-like

Noun: spaceship

Associated Words

Word	Meaning and example
space	
atmosphere	
universe	
terrestrial	
planet	
alien	
imagination	

Main Activity

Show video clips from websites such as YouTube on Roswell and UFOs.

A UFO (unidentified flying object) is a mysterious object in the sky which can't be explained by current scientific theories. UFOs are often associated with the unknown – for example, aliens from outer space.

Find out more about UFOs – the internet should help. The children should start by finding out different meanings of the word mysterious. Discuss UFO (unidentified flying object) as an example of an acronym.

Put children into groups of around three, and ask them the following questions:

- What do the letters UFO stand for?
- When does the term UFO generally date from?
- What does 'capturing the public's imagination' mean?

Children should now create two more sets of questions for the rest of the group.

Optional Activity

Debate the following, for and against:

'There is a strong case to argue that there is life outside Earth and that UFOs exist.'

Red Herring

Do some five-syllable spelling practice, using the word 'imagination':

i ma gi na tion

According to the Longman Dictionary, imagination is 'the ability to form pictures in the mind'. Examples: 'a storyteller with an incredible imagination'; 'it does not take much imagination'; 'the story captured the public imagination'.

Tip

The moon landing in 1969 is worth discussing, as there are conspiracy theories about whether it happened or not. How can it be proved? This can be very thought-provoking.

Websites

Definition of imagination – at www.ldoceonline.com

The Roswell incident – at www.youtube.com

UFOs: Roswell and elsewhere – at www.ddc.typepad.com

Dewey Decimal

001.942

34 Yellow

Colour is all around us, yet we can take it for granted and not really give it much thought. This activity aims to help the child focus on colour and be in a position to discuss different aspects of colour. This activity can be taken to different levels – a basic level for younger children, looking at the practicalities of colour and how colour is formed, to a more abstract understanding of colour and indeed how colour can be used in psychology.

By looking at the colour yellow, children have opportunities to discuss and research all aspects of this primary colour and how it affects everyday life.

Requirements

- watercolour paint in yellow, white and black
- paintbrushes
- paper
- masking tape
- scissors
- yellow highlighters/markers

Vocabulary

Verb: paint

Adjective: important

Noun: pigment

Associated Words

Word	Meaning and example
ochre	
tone	
shade	
emotion	
season	
connotation	
optimism	
clarity	

Main Activity

To begin, read the following passage aloud or allow the children to read it themselves.

The oldest yellow pigment is yellow ochre, which was amongst the first pigments used by humans. Egyptians and the ancient world made wide use of the mineral orpiment (orpiment is a deep orange-yellow colored arsenic sulfide mineral with formula As. 3. It is found in volcanic fumaroles, low temperature hydrothermal veins, and hot springs and is formed both by sublimation and as a byproduct of the decay of another arsenic mineral, realgar) for a brilliant yellow other than yellow ochre. Anything portrayed as yellow in Egyptian art generally carried this connotation.

Source: from www.webexhibits.org

First, discuss the word 'connotation' – a feeling or idea that is suggested by a particular word, although it need not be part of the word's meaning; or something suggested by an object or situation (Cambridge Dictionary).

Then discuss the colour yellow. On the one hand, yellow can stand for freshness, happiness, positivity, clarity, energy, optimism, enlightenment, remembrance, intellect, honour, loyalty and joy, but on the other, it can represent cowardice and deceit.

As a warm-up focusing exercise, issue A4 white paper marked with four triangle shapes. Using a yellow highlighter or yellow marker, the children fill in the triangles.

Ask the children to describe yellow and discuss:

- How does the colour yellow make you feel?
- What is the symbolism of the colour yellow?

Provide the text below for children to read (or read it to them):

The word yellow comes from the Old English geolu. Yellow is associated with sunshine, knowledge, and the flourishing of living creatures, but also with autumn and maturity. The yellow sun was one of humanity's most important symbols and was worshiped as God in many cultures. According to Greek mythology, the sun-god Helios wore a yellow robe and rode in a golden chariot drawn by four fiery horses across the heavenly skies. The radiant yellow light of the sun personified divine wisdom.

Source: from www.webexhibits.org

Now, ask the following questions relating to words used in the text:

- How is yellow associated with sunshine?
- What kind of knowledge do you think is being referred to?
- What does 'flourishing' mean?

Discuss the power of radiant as an adjective (sending out light; shining or glowing brightly).

Optional Activity

Name five items associated with or linked to yellow.

Paint an A3 sheet of paper, beginning with light yellow (15mm) vertical strips, progressing to dark yellow vertical strips. Allow to dry, then cut out each strip as accurately as possible. Rearrange the strips randomly and compare the effects.

Look up the following on the internet:

- Egyptians and yellow
- mummies and pyramids.

Discuss views on yellow lines and traffic – from the point of view of being instructional and environmental. How effective do you think they are? What do double yellow lines mean?

Red Herring

Vincent Van Gogh's famous 'Sunflowers' paintings used chrome yellow. The colours are now fading, and changing to a browny-green.

> Vincent Van Gogh was obsessed with the pigments in his paints, and he knew as much or more about their composition and vulnerability as many of his contemporaries. So it is a tragic irony that many of the bright red and yellow pigments that he used on his masterpieces are fading or changing color with time.
>
> Source: from https://cen.acs.org

Use the website above and find out some things about Van Gogh.

Don McLean, an American musician, wrote and sang a famous song called 'Vincent'. Look up the lyrics, and also play the YouTube recording or any other that is available. Read the lyrics while listening to the song. Discuss how effective this tune is and what impact, if any, it had on you.

Greek mythology is the body of myths and teachings that belong to the ancient Greeks, concerning their gods and heroes, the nature of the world, and the origins and significance of their own cult and ritual practices. It was a part of religion in ancient Greece. Ask the children to find out about Greek mythology, and describe it in their own words (100–200 words), or by appropriately quoting, describe what Greek mythology is. This can be handwritten or typed, depending on the child's normal way of working.

The following website might be helpful:

www.greekmythology.com

Tip

The band Coldplay had a hit single called 'Yellow'. Print out the lyrics from the internet, and ask the children to listen to the song while reading. Then discuss what the song means to them, and look at the YouTube video clip to develop the discussion.

Websites

Greek mythology – at https://en.wikipedia.org

Greek mythology website – www.greekmythology.com

Orpiment – at https://en.wikipedia.org

'Yellow' lyrics – at www.azlyrics.com

Coldplay's 'Yellow' – at www.youtube.com

Dewey Decimal

150, 750

35 Black

Children with dyslexia need a structure and often prompts and cues to complete writing exercises successfully. Prompts are usually very successful, but you may have to show how the prompt can be used, and what it means. This is very important for this activity, as the significance of the prompt may not be obvious at first to the child.

In this activity the colour 'black' is used as a prompt and children have to focus on all aspects of this colour and its significance and importance in society, both historically and culturally.

Requirements

- charcoal
- A3 paper
- tissue paper
- black card
- text (provided below)
- access to a computer and the internet

Vocabulary

Verb: blacken

Adjective: dark

Noun: black hole

Associated Words

Word	Meaning and example
black	
noir	
Dark Ages	
pitch black	
black arts	
charcoal	
coal	
shade	
black out	
blacksmith	
black-and-white photography	

Main Activity

Children could warm up by drawing ellipses (see the activity 'Ellipse' in Section 9, Part 3) or hearts, using their left and right hand, alternately. Using cotton buds or art smudgers, ask the children to vary the shades of each ellipse/heart from light to dark.

Next, show some Mitchell and Kenyon black-and-white footage, available on YouTube. Discuss how the lack of colour can affect how we see things. For example, watching a football or rugby game, it can be hard to see which team is which, depending on the strip design. If you were watching a snooker match, how would you know the colours of the balls?

Ask the children to list five things that are associated with black. For example:

- black cats (do they bring good or bad luck?)
- blackboards
- Black Friday
- Black Jack
- Black Bear
- All Blacks
- Black Death
- blackmail.

Other Meanings of Black

Ask the children to write sentences showing the different meanings as below. They can consult websites such as Wikipedia.

- Black – dark
- Black – print
- Black – Dark Ages
- Black – judges and authority
- Black – fashion
- Black – mourning
- Black – magic
- Black – evil
- Black – elegance.

Ask the children to write a text about black holes. Again, use the internet. Give them words they need to use. For example:

- stars
- cataclysms
- explosion
- fusion
- gravity
- zero volume
- dense
- energy
- cosmic objects

- planets
- horizon.

You can change these as appropriate to the age of the children.

Children may also want to look at and discuss Philip Pullman's *Northern Lights* trilogy, which describes a parallel universe.

Red Herring

The nickname of the pirate Blackbeard was derived from his thick black beard and fearsome appearance; he was reported to have tied lit fuses (slow matches) under his hat to frighten his enemies (see the earlier activity 'Pirates').

Tip

Children can make a black-to-white grid or wheel showing how gradual the shades can be. There can be many shades or just a few. Discuss how black and white can be used for contrast. For example, language is not always 'black and white'; this gives the opportunity to discuss ambiguity.

Websites

The colour black – at https://en.wikipedia.org

Learning about black with young children – at www.activityvillage.co.uk

Black holes – at www.nationalgeographic.com

Mitchell and Kenyon films – at www.youtube.com

Black things – at www.enchantedlearning.com

Dewey Decimal

150, 520, 750

36 Dodo

Children with dyslexia usually enjoy exploring and investigating; this can lead to incidental learning, which can have a positive impact on reading and writing.

The aim of this activity is to help children become more aware of the planet and how we need to preserve it. This particularly relates to wildlife and the environment in general.

Requirements

- A3 paper
- text (sample provided below)
- picture of a dodo

Vocabulary

Verb: rediscover

Adjective: flightless

Noun: dodo

Associated Words

Word	Meaning and example
extinct	
icon	
appearance	
account	
caricature	
responsible	

Main Activity

The dodo is an extinct, flightless bird that lived on the island of Mauritius, east of Madagascar, in the Indian Ocean.

Ask the children to find out about the dodo. Find expressions connected to the dodo and the connection between the dodo and *Alice in Wonderland*.

They can look at websites such as Wikipedia and answer the questions below.

Comprehension and Questions (Answers in Brackets)

- Could dodos fly? (No)
- What is the word used to describe this? (Flightless)
- What kind of bird was the Dodo? (A pigeon)
- What does extinct mean? (No longer in existence; no longer in use)
- Explain the meaning of icon. (Any person or thing that is revered – given deep respect or admiration)
- What does 'caricature' mean? (An exaggerated, usually funny, portrayal of a person or subject, their likeness being really distorted)

Optional Activity

- Find an image of the dodo, then draw and annotate the drawing (see the activity 'Annotation' in Section 11, Part 3).
- Discuss what 'landscape' means.
- Find a map with Mauritius on it. In which ocean is Mauritius located? (Indian)
- What is the name of the nearest island to Mauritius? (Reunion Island)
- Describe the dodo in not more than 50 words.

Red Herring

The term DNA (deoxyribonucleic acid) can be used for spelling practice. Break it into syllables:

DE   OXY   RIBO   NUC   LEIC (think of Leicester for the last part)

Discuss how we describe centuries. For example, the 16th century is 1500–1599.

The 16th century is regarded by historians as the century in which the rise of the West occurred. During the 16th century, Spain and Portugal explored the world's seas and opened worldwide oceanic trade routes. Large parts of the New World became Spanish and Portuguese colonies, and while the Portuguese became the masters of Asia's and Africa's Indian Ocean trade, the Spanish opened trade across the Pacific Ocean, linking the Americas with Asia.

Source: from https://en.wikipedia.org

Link and develop discussion. This helps to develop children's skills in talking and listening. For example, the above text can lead into a discussion of what piracy is, and of conflicts between sea-going powers (see earlier 'Pirates' activity).

Tip

Look up ten animals that are now extinct such as the passenger pigeon – at the time of the first settlers in North America it is believed there were almost five billion of them.

Ask the children to use the internet and find out why they became extinct. In addition, you could discuss the importance, or otherwise, of zoological attractions.

Websites

Dodo – at https://en.wikipedia.org

Top 10 extinct animals – at https://onekindplanet.org

Endangered species – at www.conserve-energy-future.com

Dewey Decimal

560, 580, 590

37 Trees

This activity aims to help the children to become more aware of the environment. By learning about trees they are also utilising investigative and problem-solving skills, as well as becoming more aware of the environment in general.

The aim is to learn about trees, the different types of products that can be made from trees, and the importance of trees for the planet.

Requirements

- a reading text (provided below)

Vocabulary

Verb: climb

Adjective: massive

Noun: oak

Associated Words

Word	Meaning and example
bark	
branch	
bud	
leaf	
trunk	
wood	
forest	
crop	
paper	
pulp	
carve	

Main Activity

Divide children into groups. Each group has to select one of the themes below and prepare a PowerPoint presentation on that theme. They will need to identify the key points of the passage below, which for ease of use has been divided into sections.

We All Need Trees

We don't just need trees to produce oxygen. They also store carbon. For centuries, we have used wood to make tools and shelter, and the provide life to many creatures. They are the biggest plants, and the longest living species on earth, and they connect us with our natural history.

Trees Are Good for our Health

Trees filter and trap air-borne pollution, making the air that we breathe cleaner. It is estimated that in one year, a tree will filter out around 1.7 kilos of pollutants! They can protect us from over-exposure to harmful rays from the sun. They can even absorb noise and provide us with a more pleasant and quiet environment. This can help with stress, and can lower blood pressure. People over the years have used trees to provide medicines, and just looking at Britain, there are over 20 species that have curative properties.

Trees Are Good for the Environment

As noted above, trees store carbon. They do this by absorbing carbon dioxide, and in doing so they can help to reduce the rate of global warming. In cities, they can provide a cooler environment by giving off moisture and reflecting heat upwards. Wooded areas will also reduce wind speeds. Trees can prevent soil erosion, and this in turn can reduce flooding.

Trees Help Wildlife

In their long lifespan, tress play host to a large number of insects and birds. They host other plants such as mosses, lichen and fungi. A mature oak tree could sustain up to 500 different species.

Trees Are Good for Communities

The environmental and health benefits of trees mean that they are a welcome feature where we live. They can bring together people who enjoy their positive qualities, and who like to be outdoors and to learn more about our natural world. They provide a wonderful playground and place of adventure for children, and adults!

Trees Are Good for the Economy

We can see that trees are beneficial and appreciated by people, and there are knock-on, economic implications. House prices are likely to be higher in an area that has mature tree growth. Workplaces benefit from the attractive environment that is produced by trees, because they can make employees feel happier.

Trees Protect the Future

So many people live in cities now – and the numbers are growing. Trees can provide the only link with nature for some people. It is vital that we respect, nurture and care for our trees, and that we protect them for future generations.

Source: adapted from www.royalparks.org.uk

Optional Activity

These comprehension questions can be presented to the whole group at the end of the activity:

- Explain why trees are vital to us all.

- How do trees benefit health?

- Can trees help the environment? If yes, give an example.

- Do trees add to improving communities? If so, why?

Add any other comments regarding trees from the above text.

Red Herring

Discuss what is meant by 'family trees'. Ask the child to look up some good examples of this. They can refer to the TV programme *Who Do You Think You Are?* by looking at Wikipedia.

Tip

If the children can find a horse chestnut tree in the locality or in any public parks, set them the task of bringing conkers back. Usually during the autumn there are lots on the ground. Provide some little planting pots and some seeding compost for the children to plant their own. They can label their pots, look after their conker and, with luck, watch it grow. A competition for the tallest mini tree can run till the Easter holidays. If at school, the children can take their trees home and plant, with permission, in their locality or gardens. These trees grow to a mighty height; alternatively, they can be planted in small containers, which will restrict their growth and give a sort of bonsai-type horse chestnut effect.

Horse Chestnut

Find out why it is called horse chestnut. Ask the children to describe the features of a horse chestnut tree. They should refer to the internet.

Websites

Family tree templates – at www.template.net

Who Do You Think You Are? TV programme – at https://en.wikipedia.org

Richmond Park – at www.royalparks.org.uk

Family tree template ideas – at www.pinterest.com

The reason it's called a horse chestnut tree – at www.countryliving.com

The conker tree – at www.youtube.com

Dewey Decimal

580, 710

38 Water

The aim of this activity is to help the children appreciate the importance of water for everyday health and wellbeing. This is another example of incidental learning, because during this activity they will be using a range of skills. This also helps with motivation. Water is an important topic, and one the children should be made aware of since water is vital for life and all living things.

Requirements

- text (provided below)

The materials required for the optional activity are:

- clear glass tumblers
- two cards, each with an arrow drawn on them
- water to drink during the activity (optional)

Vocabulary

Verb: drink

Adjective: clear

Nouns: loch, lake

Associated Words

Word	Meaning and example
steam	
sea	
distilled	
boiling point	
rain	
spring	
health	
dehydrate	
refract	
ice	

Main Activity

Water is known as H2O – that is, two parts hydrogen and one part oxygen. Water covers more than 70% of the earth's surface, and although it can be perceived as blue or grey, it is actually colourless.

Water is important for life on earth and the adult human body contains around 60% water.

The children should make up five questions from the facts about water, and test each other. They can either write this, or word-process it on a laptop. They can refer to the internet.

Optional Activity

This involves a visual illusion (see YouTube for a demonstration). Use a glass tumbler with two cards that have arrows drawn on them. Watch the arrows change direction when the glass is filled with water. You will find that when the arrow is moved a particular distance behind the glass, it looks as if it has reversed itself. This is because when light passes from one material to another, it can bend or refract.

In the experiment that you just completed, light travelled from the air, through the glass, through the water, through the back of the glass, and then back through the air, before hitting the arrow. Whenever light passes from one medium, or material, into another, it refracts.

Suggested Extension Activities for Development

- Mind-map water. Use Inspiration or an equivalent program.

Spellings to Try

- Water: Wa   ter – two syllables (see 'Spelling Corks' activity, Section 2, Part 1)
- Dehydrate: De   hy   drate – three syllables (see 'Spelling Ping-Pong' activity, Section 2, Part 1)

Red Herring

Research the following:

- sea water
- shipping/history
- canal transport
- river water – leisure/fishing/sports
- water power (steam)
- Industrial Revolution.

Tip

Drink enough water each day to keep you hydrated.

Websites

Amazing water trick – at www.youtube.com

Water – at https://en.wikipedia.org

Definition of water – at www.dictionary.com

Water facts – at www.sciencekids.co.nz

Chemistry for kids: water – at www.ducksters.com

Dewey Decimal

500, 551.3, 610

OLDHAM COUNTY PUBLIC LIBRARY

39 Circus

This activity is another example of how learning can be incidental and also fun.

Through this circus activity, children can develop a knowledge of the circus and can also find out about aspects of health and coordination. This activity can also support project work, but the fun element is the key to ensuring the child's engagement!

Requirements

- access to a computer and the internet to show archive footage
- text (provided below)

For optional activities, you will need:

- face paints or masks
- juggling balls

Vocabulary

Verb: juggle

Adjective: fearless

Noun: trapeze

Associated Words

Word	Meaning and example
big top	
clown	
acrobat	
ring master	
trapeze artist	
daredevil	
lion tamer	

animal cruelty*	
illusionist	
contortionist	
parade	
publicity	
balance	

*This can lead to a discussion on this topic.

Main Activity

Start with this definition: 'Clowns are comic performers who employ silly humour or similar types of physical comedy, often in a mime style.' Next, show clips from archive footage to introduce this activity. You can get these from YouTube.

Philip Astley created the first circus in England in 1768. See what the children can find out about Astley and his first circus.

What were the difficulties he experienced and what were the successes?

Ask the children to use the Victoria and Albert Museum website to help them: www.vam.ac.uk.

Use Wikipedia to answer the questions below (answers are given in brackets):

- What was the first circus clown act called? (Billy Buttons or the Tailor's Ride to Brentford)
- What does a tailor do? (A tailor is a person whose occupation is the making, mending or altering of clothes, especially suits, coats and other outer garments)
- What had the hired clowns to learn? (The clowns had to learn the act in which they tried to mount a horse and then got thrown off)

Ask the children to search the internet and find out about America's 'love affair' with the circus. Why is the term 'love affair' used here?

Optional Activity

Some people argue that circuses promote animal cruelty. The children should form teams and debate this. The debate question is: Should animals be banned in the circus? They need to look at the advantages and disadvantages of using animals in this way. They should research this topic using as many sources as possible.

In this debate, animal rights organisations claim that animals in captivity routinely suffer abuse and neglect. The use of animals in circuses and zoos created an incentive for poachers to hunt some animals. Those defending the circus argue that trainers love their animals and that they use positive reinforcement techniques, not punishment.

Red Herring

Ask the children if they have heard of the Indian rope trick. Search on the internet for any information about this trick and its history. Is this trick real?

Tip

Clowns can be funny, sad and scary. If resources are available, use face paint to create clown faces. In pairs, children can make each other up. Alternatively, blank masks can be provided for painting. Extension exercises can utilise drama with characters and their appearances.

Juggling is the ultimate in stress relief. When you are learning to juggle, you are immediately absorbed in the activity. It's almost impossible to think of anything but the task at hand. This makes it a great way to escape any worries, stress, hardships or anything that might be hanging over your head. For information on the benefits of juggling, search the internet.

To practise juggling, begin with two balls for coordination. Then progress to three (demonstrated on YouTube).

Websites

Historic film of circus performers – at www.youtube.com

The great Indian rope trick – at www.youtube.com

Circuses – at www.history-magazine.com

How to juggle three balls – at www.youtube.com

Benefits of juggling – at www.jugglefit.com

Dewey Decimal

790

40 Sweets

This activity covers a range of areas, and there are many teaching points here that can help children with dyslexia to develop their general knowledge and provide opportunities for the development of thinking skills. This activity will provide thought-provoking facts about how sugar is/was produced, and the role and impact of slavery. It also considers the effects on the body of consuming sugar. It looks at the range of manufacturing processes of confectionery, and therefore can touch on general science as well as health and social issues.

Requirements

- reading texts (provided below)
- A3 white paper (optional: for making a timeline of the development of sweets through the ages)

Vocabulary

Verb: taste

Adjective: fragrant

Noun: gobstopper

Associated Words

Word	Meaning and example
sucrose	
fructose	
sugar	
slavery	
health	
diabetes	
marketing	

confectionery	
chewy	
boiled	
sweet tooth	
fruit	

Main Activity

Start with the following passage for comprehension:

The History of Sweets

The earliest sweet, which people have eaten since prehistoric times, was honey. The origins of confectionery can be traced back to about 2000 BC to the ancient Egyptians, who made sweets by combining fruits and nuts with honey. The Romans, Greeks and Chinese made sweets with sesame seeds.

Source: from www.candyhistory.net

Penny Tray

The 'penny tray' in the UK afforded children the opportunity to spend pocket/snack money on a small item or items from a tray. Generally, sweet/grocer shops would operate near schools to capitalise on this market. Check out the websites of some of the snacks available in the 1960s. There is scope here for making up a memory quiz of, say, 20 items.

Refer to the YouTube video of 1960s sweets from *The Toffs in the Tenement*. Children can find out different meanings of the word 'toffs' and also find out what a tenement is. They can also use other websites for information.

Natural Sugars

Find out what the best natural substitutes for sugar are.

Look at the internet for a start, then ask the children to write an argument for and against the use of sugar substitutes (they can do this in pairs). They will need to research this further themselves. Points to consider include taste, cost, health benefits, availability and appeal!

Sugar and Slavery

Slave trading was part of a highly profitable triangle of trade that spanned the Atlantic. Manufactured goods were traded to the West African coast for slaves, who were shipped to the sugar colonies (via the infamous Middle Passage), and sugar, molasses and rum were shipped from the islands to England.

Ask the children to produce a timeline of slavery and the dates of abolition of slavery. The internet could be useful here.

Chocolate/Candy

Chocolate/candy is a great topic for a project, and children can make up a PowerPoint presentation on this. With approval, they can share chocolate/candy bars with their peers while watching/listening to the presentation; this makes the experience more memorable.

Packaging History

Ask the children to find out about the history of candy packaging and draw an annotated timeline of the types of packaging in candy from pre-1900 to the present day. Wikipedia can help, but they should research it more extensively.

Optional Activity

This tasting exercise involves planning, designing and writing.

Invent a new sweet and list its ingredients. Design an amazing wrapper with a sales pitch/text, explaining why everyone should buy this sweet. Discuss existing products and their texts. Have an imaginary tasting session with these amazing new creations.

Red Herring

Discuss how sweet substances can lead to teeth cavities, using any relevant websites, or reference books.

An interesting anecdote is that the ancient Greek philosopher Aristotle first observed that sweet foods like soft figs caused tooth decay, but nobody believed him. Can you imagine why no one believed him?

Tip

With agreement and support from parents, children can make up a tray bake of their choice; finding a recipe, purchasing ingredients and baking are all part of the process. This is also a great way of fundraising for any charities throughout the year. A sugary positive!

Websites

The sweet history of sweets – at www.candyhistory.net

Candy – at https://en.wikipedia.org

Sugar and slavery – at clements.umich.edu

Sugar plantations in the Caribbean – at https://en.wikipedia.org

Natural subsitutes for sugar – at www.mindbodygreen.com

History of slavery – at www.reuters.com

Dewey Decimal

610, 760

41 Stunts

A useful aim in dealing with children with dyslexia is to help them look more deeply at what they are reading or watching. They can be inclined to take some things literally, so any exercise that helps them to look beneath the surface to investigate how certain events occurred is extremely useful. This is the case in this activity on stunts. Stunts in movies are now becoming extremely sophisticated, and seemingly impossible events and activities can take place in a movie. It is useful for the child with dyslexia to find out how this can happen.

The aim of this activity is to research and discuss what stunts are and how effective and memorable they can be, when used in film, drama and media presentation, and also how dangerous they may be.

Requirements

- access to a computer and internet to show video clips

Vocabulary

Verb: engage

Adjective: spectacular

Noun: stunt

Associated Words

Word	Meaning and example
spectacular	
stunt	
daring	
dangerous	
publicity	
elaborate	
parachute	
skilled	
audacious	

Main Activity

Watch one or both of the YouTube video clips described below (the Felix clip is longer). The build-up of tension is excellent, and there is a detailed narrative of sequential importance, as Felix is supported by ground control when he undertakes this jump.

A stunt is an exciting action, usually in a film, which is dangerous or appears dangerous and usually needs to be done by someone skilled: a typical action movie has plenty of spectacular stunts. A stunt is also something interesting that is done in order to attract attention and get publicity for the person or company responsible for it. Advertising can involve a variety of stunts.

YouTube Video Clips

Search for the link of stuntman Gary Connery jumping from a helicopter at 730 metres (2,400 feet), flying a wingsuit. Guess how many cardboard boxes Gary used for his landing strip.

The second clip you should search for shows Felix Baumgartner freefalling, after flying to an altitude of 39,045 metres (128,100 feet) in a helium-filled balloon. What was the fastest speed Felix reached in his descent?

Eight Tips for Stunt Success

Search for this on the internet, and put the eight tips in order from most important to least important. Ask the children to give reasons for their choice.

Group challenges: working together in a team, discuss and plan an imaginative stunt to promote a product or any other thing. Use the eight tips for stunt success.

Optional Activity

WARNING! This is an optional task. It involves reading about and watching some dangerous stunts, and some of them can go horribly wrong. Search websites such as YouTube.

How Do You Become a Stunt Performer?

Learn about becoming a stunt performer and what it takes to become a stunt performer, with career details and course listings from professional stunt organisations.

Red Herring

Discuss the saying 'to pull a stunt or a hoax' (to carry out a trick, deception or practical joke (against someone)).

April Fools' Day

April Fools' Day is celebrated every year on 1 April by playing practical jokes and spreading hoaxes. The jokes, and their victims, are called April Fools. People playing April Fools' jokes expose their prank by shouting 'April Fool!' Some newspapers, magazines and other published media report fake stories, which can appear topical and credible.

Look at Wikipedia for information about the spaghetti-tree hoax! This is a good task for reading practice – the spaghetti-tree hoax was only a three-minute broadcast on TV, but it has become very famous and is still well known today. It came from a BBC *Panorama* report in 1957! But the clue to its fame lies on the day it was broadcast – 1 April! Although spaghetti is a common meal in homes and restaurants today, back in 1957 this was not the case and few people in the UK were familiar with the ingredients of spaghetti.

Mini Task

Find out exactly what spaghetti is made from.

How did the BBC dream up this April Fools' stunt? Why did the British people believe the story? Why do you think CNN called it 'the biggest news hoax ever'?

Once children have completed this task they can look at the actual video of the hoax on YouTube.

With the advent of the internet and readily available global news services, April Fools' pranks can catch and embarrass a wider audience than ever before.

Tip

Search for interesting websites that provide tips for great stunts.

Websites

Definition of stunt – at https://dictionary.cambridge.org

April Fools' Day – at https://en.wikipedia.org

Publicity stunts – at www.thedrum.com

Ten of history's most death defying stunts – at www.popularmechanics.com

Failed stunts – at www.youtube.com

How to become a stunt performer – at www.hotcourses.com

Deadly circus stunts – at mentalfloss.com

Tips for great stunts – at www.sharpperformanceconsulting.com

Dewey Decimal

790

Comprehension

42 What's New/Interesting/ Forgettable?

Children with dyslexia often spend a great deal of time decoding print, but this may be at the expense of comprehension. As a result they may comprehend the text in a literal and perhaps superficial way, and not access the deeper meaning of the text. Interpreting text critically is an important aspect of comprehension, and particularly identifying inferences and the deeper meaning of the text. It is important that children with dyslexia are encouraged to do this as a habit, and not just take the text literally.

This activity aims to help develop critical comprehension skills at all levels.

Requirements

- newspapers
- large sheets of art paper

Vocabulary

Verb: print

Adjective: latest

Noun: periodical

Associated Words

Word	Meaning and example
edition	
press	
compose	
classified	
feature	
media	

Main Activity

Children should work in groups of two or three. Provide each group with a newspaper (it can be an old one), then follow this process:

1. The children take a piece of art paper – large enough to be pinned on the wall.

2. Ask the children to divide the paper into three columns:

    - new

    - interesting

    - forgettable.

3. They then read through the newspaper and cut out pieces that can be inserted into each of the categories.

4. In their notebooks they write the heading or first sentence of each of the articles, and then, very importantly, they have to justify their choice. In other words, they need to say why the article falls into that particular column.

5. Children then give an oral presentation to the rest of the group on their choices.

Optional Activity

Try to arrange a visit to the sub-editor's offices of a local newspaper. It is there that articles are discarded or decisions are made to print and where in the paper the article should go. If it is not possible to arrange a visit, it might be possible to organise a Skype interview with a sub-editor or send a few representatives to the newspaper office to interview a sub-editor.

Red Herring

What role have newspapers played during important periods in history (e.g. during the Second World War)? Ask the children to investigate this and find out what is meant by censorship.

Dewey Decimal

070

43 Time

Understanding and utilising concepts can be challenging for children with dyslexia. Once they have a fuller conceptual understanding of what they are learning, their skills in that area can escalate. This can be noted in maths, but it also applies across other subjects too. The concept of time is an important one for children with dyslexia. Often, one of their learning issues is that they do not have a good awareness of time. This can, of course, get them into all sorts of bother!

The aim of this activity is to help to develop a fuller appreciation and use of time devices and how time is an essential aspect of daily life. This activity can also help in the understanding of verb tenses – past, present and future.

Requirements

- a wristwatch or smartphone
- a wall clock (analogue)

Vocabulary

Verb: measure

Adjective: accurate

Noun: clock

Associated Words

Word	Meaning and example
duration	
measurement	
precise	
compare	
sequence	
past	
countdown	

watch	
present	

Main Activity

Engage the group in a discussion on the topic of time. Start with different types of clocks (digital and analogue). For example, a digital clock is a type of clock that displays the time digitally (i.e. in numerals or other symbols). An analogue clock is a type of clock where the time is indicated by the positions of clockwise-rotating hands.

Provide a definition of time (see below). A point of time is measured in hours and minutes past midnight or noon. You could include a discussion of past, present and future – tenses of existence.

Time is also a component quantity of various measurements, used to sequence events, to compare the duration of events or the intervals between them.

Time is defined as the duration in which all things happen, or a precise instant that something happens. An example of historical time is the Renaissance period (art) era.

An example of time is breakfast at eight o'clock in the morning.

A timetable (a table of time) measures classes during the day and week – controlling your time during the day.

Time Facts

For hundreds of years, people used burning candles, dripping water – known as water clocks – or sifting sand to tell time's passage. People still use sand clocks or hourglasses to keep time.

In the 14th century, Europeans developed basic clocks with springs and weights. These clocks sounded a bell every hour. Later, clock makers developed the hour and minute hands. These clocks were not very accurate.

Source: from http://easyscienceforkids.com

Discuss with the group some expressions using time. For example:

- the time of your life – signifies enjoyment
- 'Time up!' (e.g. in a quiz such as *Mastermind*)
- extra time (e.g. at the end of a game; also used for timed examinations)
- just in time

- timely intervention
- if I only had time
- half-time
- full-time
- time to decide
- real time
- time will tell (discuss personification)
- what's the time?
- time to go
- there's a time for everything
- 'Who Knows Where the Time Goes?' (see below).

Optional Activity

Talk about time travel, referring to the science fiction genre – for example, use a YouTube clip from *Doctor Who*.

Watch or discuss the film *Back to the Future*. How likely is it that time travel has been invented already? If it was, would people from the past, or aliens, be here now? This could be done in the form of a debate.

Look at syllabification and spellings:

Duration: Du   ra   tion

Measurement: Meas   ure   ment

Red Herring

Discuss the Renaissance period of art, and how long it lasted.

The High Renaissance. High Renaissance art, which flourished (developed) for about 35 years, from the early 1490s to 1527, when Rome was sacked (destroyed) by imperial troops, revolved (circled) around three towering (huge) figures: Leonardo da Vinci (1452–1519), Michelangelo (1475–1564), and Raphael (1483–1520).

Source: from www.all-art.org

Provide examples of images related to the above passage for discussion.

The folk song 'Who Knows Where the Time Goes?' by Fairport Convention focuses on time. Look at the YouTube video clip of this song and print out the lyrics for this song for discussion.

Tip

Is Time an Illusion?

Of course, the moment during which you read that sentence is no longer happening. This one is. In other words, it feels as though time flows, in the sense that the present is constantly updating itself. We have a deep intuition that the future is open, until it becomes present, and that the past is fixed.

Websites

Time Monsters – at www.timemonsters.com

Doctor Who clip – at www.youtube.com

Fairport Convention, 'Who Knows Where the Time Goes?' – at www.youtube.com

Facts about time – at www.buzzfeed.com

Dewey Decimal

600

44 Volcanoes

Every opportunity needs to be used to develop reading comprehension. One of the key points that needs to be considered is ensuring the material engages the child and is of some interest. In other words, it will prompt the child to find out more about the topic.

For this activity, we are using the topic of volcanoes. This topic can touch on a number of subjects, including language, art and science, and there can be much children can find out for themselves about the topic. This can lead to independent learning.

The aim of this activity is to develop reading comprehension and follow-up discussion. One of the activities includes the construction of a homemade volcano, which can be a simple but fun activity. This scientific experiment helps the children to follow a sequenced plan and utilise teamwork skills in order to achieve a simulation of a volcanic eruption.

Requirements

- text (example provided below)

The ingredients for the optional activity of making each model of a volcano are below (refer to the website noted below for more detailed information):

- 1 x plastic 1-litre bottle (e.g. a recycled milk container), plain, or painted for effect
- funnel for filling bottle
- 6 cups of flour
- 2 cups of salt
- 4 tablespoons of cooking oil
- warm water
- dishwashing detergent
- food colouring (yellow and red, or orange)
- 2 tablespoons of baking soda
- a paper tissue
- white vinegar
- if indoors, use old newspapers and a baking dish to protect surfaces

Vocabulary

Verb: erupt

Adjective: catastrophic

Noun: magma

Associated Words

Word	Meaning and example
Vesuvius	
force	
lava	
Pompeii	
eruption	

gas	
catastrophe	

Main Activity

Start by showing the trailer for the film *Pompeii* from YouTube.

Children should read the following for practice in analysis and comprehension:

The eruption of Mount Vesuvius in 79 AD was one of the most catastrophic volcanic eruptions in European history.

- A volcano is a mountain that erupts.

- Rock under the earth's surface is so hot that it melts. This melted rock is called magma.

- Erupting magma is called lava.

- Volcanoes become bigger every time they erupt as the lava cools and makes a new layer of rock.

- Volcanoes can erupt under water and form new islands from the cooled lava.

- Volcanoes can be found on the moon and on other planets.

- There are more than 500 active volcanoes on Earth.

Optional Activity

Making a Volcano

If indoors, use a baking dish (for placing the bottle/volcano on), and spread old newspapers to protect surfaces. For an option with less mess, use an outside location.

The materials for this are listed above.

First, add the following, in order, to the plastic bottle:

- 6 cups of flour

- 2 cups of salt

- 4 tablespoons of cooking oil

- warm water as required

- 6 drops of dishwashing detergent

- food colouring (yellow and red, or orange).

Then fold 2 tablespoons of baking soda into a tissue and drop it into the bottle.

Next, slowly pour a half a cup of white vinegar into the bottle.

The detergent helps trap the bubbles produced by the reaction, so you get better lava. The cool red lava is the result of a chemical reaction between the baking soda and vinegar. In this reaction, carbon dioxide gas is produced. This is present in real volcanoes. As the carbon dioxide gas is produced, pressure builds up inside the plastic bottle, until the gas bubbles (thanks to the detergent) out of the 'volcano'.

Red Herring

Discuss another type of natural disaster – the tsunami. A tsunami, or tidal wave, also known as a seismic sea wave, is a series of waves in a water body caused by the displacement of a large volume of water, generally in an ocean or a large lake.

Tip

To make a volcano more authentic, children can cover their bottle with torn newspaper, glued on with PVA adhesive and painted when dried. This part could be carried out beforehand, and children could use their own bottles, allowing for many eruptions and comparisons.

Websites

How to make an erupting volcano – at https://science.wonderhowto.com

Homemade volcano – at www.learning4kids.net

Pompeii trailer – at www.youtube.com

Dewey Decimal

551.2

45 Critical Thinking

As indicated in Activity 42, children with dyslexia focus too heavily on reading accuracy, and this can be at the expense of reading comprehension. Yet reading comprehension is vital for developing learning and thinking skills, and obtaining pleasure from the reading activity.

The aim of this activity is to develop children's comprehension and thinking skills. Critical thinking is a crucial area, as it helps to solve problems, make decisions, ask questions, construct plans, evaluate ideas, organise information and create objects. These can all provide the child with dyslexia with a sense of accomplishment and add considerably to their learning skills.

Requirements

- text (provided below)
- examples for discussion (provided below)

Vocabulary

Verb: think

Adjective: imaginative

Noun: thought

Associated Words

Word	Meaning and example
critical	
observation	
interpretation	
creative	
reflection	
organisation	
evaluation	
inference	
question	
mental	
decision	
construct	

Main Activity

What is thinking all about? It is:

- the act or practice of somebody who thinks, a thought
- a way of reasoning: judgement (e.g. 'to my thinking, this is not a good idea')
- the skills we need for critical thinking.

The skills that we need in order to be able to think critically are varied, and include observation, analysis, interpretation, reflection, evaluation, inference, explanation, problem solving and decision making.

Search the internet for information about developing critical thinking skills. The task is to get the children into pairs and they need to try to teach each other how to think critically.

To help them, ask them to study tips such as:

Pause and wait, don't intervene immediately, ask open-ended questions and encourage critical thinking in new and different ways.

They should take a passage from a reader or a topic they are working on, and use this as a basis for the task.

Then, using the internet, ask the children to note 15 examples of how critical thinking can be used. It is a good idea to suggest some – such as a soccer coach, police detective, parents budgeting money, a creative writer and someone in charge of road safety.

Optional Activity

Log on to Pinterest and select 'Got 5 Minutes'. Download and print out the activity. Discuss this first, then complete the activity.

Ask the children to find and save any ideas about critical thinking activities on Pinterest. There are also more ideas on critical thinking available by searching 'thinking skills', 'Bloom's taxonomy verbs' and 'think education'.

Red Herring

Check out 'Think Tank' for youngsters. There is a site for sharing creative writing and storytelling called 'Underlined' (previously known as 'Figment'). Here is a statement from their website:

Figment is getting Underlined! While the Figment site is shutting down, the community will still have a home to continue telling amazing stories. On Underlined, contributors will still be able to create, comment on, and discuss stories, upload covers, edit their work, and more! Figment loves the passion and creativity of the Figment community, and are excited to introduce the new platform.

Source: from http://bigthink.com

Tip

'Critical Thinking Basic' is an app that aims to help users to assess and improve their quality of reasoning. It asks the user to reflect about the reasoning behind an issue they are working on, and guide their reflection process through nine simple 'Universal Standards of Reasoning'. This can be used if they are working on an important issue where for instance they might have to:

- explain a point of view or thought, or make a request
- communicate a decision or an idea
- assess or make a recommendation for a solution, product or service
- teach or learn a subject
- help someone to make up their mind.

Dingbats is a great game to play which can help develop critical thinking. A junior version is also available.

Websites

A think tank for creative teens – at http://bigthink.com

Problem-solving activities – at www.brighthorizons.com

Fifteen positive examples of critical thinking – at www.insightassessment.com

Dingbats – www.dingbats.net

Dewey Decimal

150

46 Celebrity 'Mastermind'

Children with dyslexia often have difficulties with memory. Two key factors in relation to memory are 'comprehension' and 'retelling'. If the materials are comprehended, then there is a greater chance of recall. Also, if the child has an opportunity to respond orally, either through discussion or in a quiz-type situation, then the chances are that retention will be even greater.

'Mastermind' is a good example of a quiz, as contenders have the opportunity to answer questions on their specialist topic. This means they have an idea of the type of questions that may be asked, and should also be familiar with the content area.

The aim of this activity is to help children to learn and retain materials, and develop reading comprehension. Additionally, as the group will be fielding the questions, they will also have to consider what questions to ask.

Requirements

- background reading (provided below)
- a timer
- a prize
- access to a computer to show a video example of the game (optional)

Vocabulary

Verb: deliberate

Adjective: cunning

Noun: time-keeper

Associated Words

Word	Meaning and example
specialist	
pass	
participation	
championship	

depth	
bank of questions	

Main Activity

Look at a YouTube example of the 'Mastermind' quiz programme to become familiar with the programme format.

'Mastermind' has an interesting history. The former journalist Magnus Magnusson was the first Question Master, and became closely associated with the programme. Although it was first shown late at night, it rose in popularity and was shifted to peak viewing hours. Children can look at the history of 'Mastermind' on the internet and answer the questions:

- What is the object of the game?
- What is the importance of the black leather chair?
- What does 'Pass' mean in this context?
- What did the Question Master say if he had started asking a question, and the time bell rang?

One of the popular components of 'Mastermind' is the 'Specialist Subject' section. In this section, the contestant has to select a specialist subject and answer questions on it. Ask the children what their specialist subject would be. Get them in pairs to ask each other questions about their specialist subjects.

This is a celebrity version of 'Mastermind', so the difference is that each group (they can work in pairs on this one) chooses to be a celebrity. One of the specialist topics will be on that celebrity. The other will be on a topic that each group selects for themselves.

The questions will be compiled by the group. Give them several weeks to read up about the celebrity and the topic, but they should decide at the start who their celebrity will be and their topics.

The children then get the instructions and can become familiar with the 'Mastermind' format.

After several weeks, start the 'Mastermind' rounds. Select the order for the contestants; this might be random.

Remember that you will need a time-keeper – two minutes is the 'Mastermind' norm, but you can extend this to five minutes for each topic.

Operate the same format as 'Mastermind', with rounds, semi-finals and a final. The winning group will receive a prize.

Optional Activity

If this activity is being done at a school, discuss with the headteacher and perhaps the finalists or semi-finalists. Winners can appear at the assembly with the whole school asking the questions. These should be prepared and vetted in advance.

Red Herring

One of the unique features of 'Mastermind' is that there is no money prize – the prize is a trophy.

In some game shows contestants donate their prize money to charity. Ask the children to make a list of game shows that donate money to charity. This is an opportunity to look at different charities and what each of them do. Each group can select one charity, and describe the work of that charity and where they get the funds.

Websites

'Mastermind' – at www.bbc.co.uk

Subjects banned on 'Mastermind' – at www.theguardian.com

Charity Commission – at www.gov.uk

Dewey Decimal

030

Learning Games for Fun

47 Pictures Say 100 Words

It is important to help the young person with dyslexia to access as rich a vocabulary as possible – often there is a significant discrepancy between oral vocabulary and written vocabulary. They often know the words that can be used in the written piece, but are unable to access the word when required. This can cause frustration and feelings of failure. One of the aims of this book is to help the child to generate a richer vocabulary.

Requirements

- downloaded and printed pictures from the internet
- smartphone or camera for children to take photos (optional)
- printer for children's photos (optional)

Vocabulary

Verb: observe

Adjective: colourful

Noun: picture

Associated Words

Word	Meaning and example
detail	
paint	
outline	
mass	
merge	
background	

Main Activity

Children should work in small groups. First, each group has to select a picture. You can take a virtual tour of the National Gallery at their website: www.nationalgallery.org.uk

Children should then make a list of 100 words from that picture. To help them remember where they are on the picture, they should print out a copy of the picture and follow the steps below:

- Divide the picture into squares – perhaps 16 squares.
- Code each square in the same way as a map.
- Try to get 100 words, and note the square each word refers to.

Optional Activity

Children can take their own pictures of interesting landscape views outside. They should try to avoid taking pictures of people. They could also exchange photos with a partner, and do the same task again with their partner's picture.

Red Herring

Access the internet and gather information about a famous photographer – it can be any kind of photographer such as the rock/pop photographer Bob Gruen. His website is: www.bobgruen.com

Dewey Decimal

740, 750

48 Share for Success – 'Helping Me, Helping You'

Children with dyslexia tend to work more effectively through interactive learning. This means they will benefit from working in groups. It is important that they get the opportunity not only to work in groups but to be a key member of the group. Although they may have difficulties in some aspects of learning, they may well have abilities in others. For example, they may be able to think 'outside the box' and see a line of reasoning that others in the group do not see. It is important that they are afforded this opportunity. Some care therefore must be taken to consider how the groups are constructed, to make sure that dyslexic children do not feel overwhelmed by the group and that they feel sufficiently comfortable in the group to volunteer information and confident enough to support others in the group.

The aim of this activity is to develop peer learning and constructive collaboration. This will be very useful for the child with dyslexia and provide opportunities to enhance self-esteem and confidence.

Requirements

- paper and pencil for taking notes
- smartphones or digital recorders (optional) for recording notes

Vocabulary

Verb: assist

Adjective: collaborative

Noun: peer

Associated Words

Word	Meaning and example
discussion	
communicate	
support	
teamwork	

Main Activity

Below are lists of tasks or problems. The children work in pairs to tackle these problems. They need to record or note the steps they used, and at the end they have to assess how helpful it was to work in pairs. They should then reflect on how they can work better together. What could they do differently?

Some suggested tasks are below; children can add some of their own:

- build a bridge
- make the home safer

- protect the environment
- start a café.

Optional Activity

Select members of the group to be observers and make comments on how the pair were working – looking at the good points and also where improvements can be made.

Red Herring

There are a number of TV programmes that involve team games – where the team have to work together. Choose and watch some of these; identify the parts of the activity where teamwork was evident.

Dewey Decimal

302, 303

49 We've Got Talent

It is well established that learning is more effective when it is fun and everyone participates. The child with dyslexia responds more effectively when the activity is interactive. Group work can therefore be good practice for children with dyslexia, and can be beneficial for all children in the group. Activities are more effective if the child has some background knowledge and understanding – for example, if it is modelled on a popular television show or a popular game that they are familiar with.

The aim of this activity, which is modelled on a television talent show, is to help children to participate – perhaps even outside their own comfort zone – in a collaborative group activity. As well as the pleasure and fun element, the activity aims to develop imagination, self-esteem, oral vocabulary and collaborative group work.

Requirements

- video-recorder or equivalent
- after the first week, children will be performing in small groups for a talent show, and they will need access to any equipment they might need for this

Vocabulary

Verb: entertain

Adjective: talented

Noun: performer

Associated Words

Word	Meaning and example
competition	
judge	
participation	
audience	
voting	
compere	

Main Activity

Before you start, the whole group needs to appoint a compere who will introduce all of the acts, and a panel of three judges. The activity can then be carried out in pairs or small groups of three or four. It is based on a talent competition, and each group or pair has to undertake a performance. It is best to do this in groups so that everyone is able to participate. Within a group, there is scope for individual performances.

The children will need some time for preparation – this can take place over a number of weeks, allocating time for this each week. For example, a six-week plan (one hour per week) is shown below:

- Week 1 – watch some YouTube clips of talent show performances (e.g. from *Britain's Got Talent* or *America's Got Talent*). In groups, develop some ideas for a performance.

- Week 2 – practice and rehearsal. The groups can find their own space to work. Try to keep all the groups in separate spaces. They can then practise their act in private.

- Week 3 – the compere introduces all the acts in turn. Each group has to do a four-minute performance, and at the end of each the judges make a comment. Each child receives three voting slips with the name of each act except their own. During the coming week, they have to select four acts they want to go through to the next round.

- Week 4 – the results. The compere announces the results, and names the four acts with the most votes who will appear in the finals. All the runners-up are thanked and complimented on their act. The four finalist acts then have one week to rehearse a different version of their act for the finals.

- Week 5 – the finals. All four acts then perform and the judges comment. This should be video-recorded. All children, except the finalists, are then given a voting slip. During the coming week, they have to record their vote in secret into a ballot box.

- Week 6 – the grand final. Results for the four acts are given, and the two with the highest score are through to the grand final. They have one hour to practise their act for the grand final. During that time, the whole group can watch a video recording of the semi-final – the last four, and particularly the final two. The final two then perform their act, and the judges comment. All children (except the finalists) are given voting slips and have to record their vote immediately. The compere then reads the final tally. The winner is announced, and they do an encore. The runner-up is praised and thanked.

Optional Activity

Imagine the six-week show was on television. You have to be a TV critic, and write an account of the show, commenting on some of the performances. Be kind!

Red Herring

Many singers and entertainers have become very famous after appearing on a TV talent show. Find out about a previous winner or finalist, and make a list of their accomplishments and challenges, and where they are now. The information could be presented as a timeline.

Dewey Decimal

790, 791, 792

50 Self-Portrait

Positive self-esteem is crucial for children to become effective learners. Games and fun activities are excellent for this. Children have to focus on their own face, and produce a self-portrait drawing of their face. It is important to make this light-hearted and fun. It is also important for all children to complete the task and obtain positive feedback from the activity.

The aim is to look at the process of observing, focusing and sequencing information. To some children, the tasks may seem quite ambitious, but by going through the steps and the sequence, they can achieve success.

Requirements

- paper
- small mirrors
- pencils or charcoal
- an eraser
- a clipboard
- oval templates (plain paper printed with oval shapes to guide drawing, or cut-out ovals)
- access to a computer and internet (optional)

Vocabulary

Verb: look

Adjective: smiley

Noun: face

Associated Words

Word	Meaning and example
observe	
draw	
focus	

ellipse	
symmetrical	
balance	

Main Activity

It is a good idea to start with a warm-up activity. On a large sheet of paper, the children take a pencil and, using a continuous line, fill the page. Within this doodle/scribble, various shapes can appear. You should then encourage the children to develop these by making them more definitive. For example, there may be a bird shape, an image of a figure/monster, or a car/vehicle. This exercise also helps develop imagination. It also helps with relaxation, so it does not matter if no shapes can be found. Children can also swap hands, and draw on the other side of the paper. It is interesting to note that children often do not have the same expectation in terms of drawing skill from the non-favoured hand, and results can be very rewarding.

You should then introduce the topic of self-portraiture. As an option, children could watch a YouTube clip on 'How to Draw a Quick, Simple and Easy Self-Portrait.'

They can follow this by creating their drawing on a blank A4 sheet if they prefer. Otherwise, you should issue templates – a blank oval and an oval with ellipses marked to help position features. Children can choose to use either, or both.

Children will be in their own work spaces, and each will have a small mirror. You then provide them with a template, and ask them to try to draw their faces using the template as a guide. You may find that many children will say, 'I can't draw.' It is important not to pressure them if they are reluctant, as this is not conducive to good learning practice. But with encouragement and perhaps having someone in the group to model the exercise, they will usually make an attempt.

Optional Activity

Issue children with large photocopied images of faces (magazines are a great source for these). Then annotate the photocopied portrait and describe all features – emotions, smile lines, grimaces.

Ask them how many facial muscles they think we have. They can check this on the internet.

Work from a number of mixed photocopied images of faces. Tear up three or four of them and mix the scraps together. Now, assemble a face using the scraps and glue them on an A4 sheet as a montage. This will result in the creation of some really interesting faces.

Red Herring

Simulate a 'pretend' identity parade. Introduce the topic of what an identity parade is, and who would do this. Discuss the reasons and purposes. Reflect on which features would help to identify the character(s).

Tip

Warm up the children's drawing skills by asking them to doodle, then to draw 'Lazy Eights'.

Websites

Self-portrait projects for children – at www.hellowonderful.co

How to draw a self-portrait – at www.youtube.com

Dewey Decimal

743

51 Quizzes

Most children like some form of competition. Quizzes are a fun form of learning and can be very enjoyable, with the children adding to their knowledge without realising it. Using a variety of quizzes that cover all topics, new vocabulary can be introduced and existing topics can be revised. This can be a useful activity prior to and after the main study of a topic.

The aim of this activity is to extend children's knowledge and vocabulary, and to introduce a fun element to their learning. You can also help children to make up their own quizzes, and to structure questions.

Requirements

The requirements for the main activity include a selection of age-appropriate quizzes which link to the curriculum. In the UK, you could access Dorling Kindersley (www.dk.com) materials for subject-specific quizzes. Web searches can be made for other quizzes.

Vocabulary

Verb: question

Adjective: specific

Noun: quiz (this can also be a verb)

Associated Words

Word	Meaning and example
clue	
questioning	
create	
equivalent	
request	
appropriate	
relevant	
nonsense	

Main Activity

Begin by showing children a YouTube video clip such as 'Top 15 Unbelievable and Amazing (Interesting) Facts'.

You could use the smartboard, or equivalent, and ask the children to take turns in reading out the facts as they are displayed. This can help the child to memorise their particular fact as they verbalise them. Children are generally happy to join in, and this is great for developing reading skills. The image can be paused to allow for harder sentences to be read, and this supports the child's confidence.

The children should try to remember as many of the images and as much of the subject content as they can. They should try to remember the text by focusing on the key words used. The aim is to see how much of the overall slides, images, colour, content and information they can recall. Answers can be written down, and the exercise can be timed or untimed.

To finish the session, use Dorling Kindersley quiz cards, or a similar resource; get the children to take turns reading the questions and answers at the end, for practice.

Optional Activity

Why You Should Make a Quiz

Create a quiz to make learning more interactive and engaging. It has been shown in research that regular quizzes (not to be graded or evaluated – this is key) boost memory retention, drive engagement and make learning fun. Children can follow a modelled example to make up their own quizzes.

Red Herring

How the Word 'Quiz' Came to Be

It is interesting to think of the origins of words. Ask the children if they can guess the origins of the word 'quiz.'

Once they have tried to work it out themselves, give them some cues and ask them to write a précis of the origins of the word quiz.

Children can try to come up with a new word for something – discuss how words are chosen for meaning.

Tip

Use a quiz timer device for dramatic effects and to enhance the activity. These are freely available on the internet.

Websites

Where did that word come from? – at www.theguardian.com

Quizzes – at www.kidzworld.com

Quizzes for kids – at www.pinterest.com

50 fun questions to get your kid talking – at www.parents.com

Online quiz creator – www.onlinequizcreator.com

Origins of the word 'quiz' – at https://en.oxforddictionaries.com

Online timers – at www.pinterest.co.uk

Dewey Decimal

030

52 Superstitions

The aim of this activity is for children to become aware of different cultural norms and superstitions. It is best to keep this as a fun activity and to make it as light-hearted as possible. We can learn a lot about cultures and the habits of previous generations through investigating the different superstitions they held. This activity can be seen as information gathering, acquiring cultural and historical information.

Requirements

- text for discussion (provided below)

For one of the optional activities, you will need:

- a needle
- thread
- a cork

Vocabulary

Verb: demonstrate

Adjectives: sinister, lucky

Noun: charms

Associated Words

Word	Meaning and example
omen	
belief	
credible	
supernatural	
irrational	
ominous	

Main Activity

Start with a definition of superstition. For example:

> Superstition is a pejorative term for any belief or practice that is considered irrational: for example, if it arises from ignorance, a misunderstanding of science or causality, a positive belief in fate or magic, or fear of that which is unknown. Superstition also refers to religious beliefs or actions arising from irrationality.
>
> Source: from https://en.wikipedia.org

What are superstitions? Discuss some examples of superstition. For example:

- Black cats – are you doomed to bad luck if a black cat crosses your path? This depends which country you are in. In what country is a black cat considered lucky?
- Mirrors – if you break a mirror, will you have seven years of bad luck?
- Ladders – it is said that walking under a ladder can be bad luck.

Invite more examples from the children. Some people always wear or bring a particular item of clothing or a good-luck charm to help them or their team win.

Syllabification

Break some of the words provided above into syllables and have a discussion on vocabulary/spelling patterns:

- o   mens
- be   lief
- cred   i   ble
- su   per   nat   u   ral
- ir   ra   tion   al
- charms
- su   per   sti   tion

Optional Activity

Take a threaded needle and pierce it into the centre of one end of a cork. Ask two of the children to demonstrate this activity. One child dangles the cork over the head of the other child, who is sitting. The cork should be completely steady to begin. After a short time, the cork should move back and forward if the child sitting is male and move in a circular motion if the child is female. Over the years this superstitious activity has been used to determine the gender of an unborn baby; a wedding ring has been used instead of a cork.

Children can read and discuss the following passage:

Four Major Reasons Why People Believe in Superstitions

Superstitions are everywhere. From the chain messages that ask you to 'forward this to 10 people and something good will happen in the next 24 hours' to your uncle who thinks that his favorite sports team didn't win because he wasn't wearing his 'lucky' hat, superstitious behavior may well be considered the hallmark of human nature.

After all, we don't see other animals wearing their lucky hats or chanting mantras when they try to hunt, forage, look for a mate or protect themselves from danger. They just do their thing.

Source: from www.psychmechanics.com

Red Herring

What rhymes with 'omens'? Romans. Find out some facts about Roman superstitions.

Can you find words that rhyme with superstition? Use a dictionary to help with this.

Discuss the following three-syllable words:

- ad   di   tion
- am   bi   tion
- nu   tri   tion
- ma   gi   cian
- tra   di   tion

Tip

Halloween is a great time for this activity!

Websites

Tony Robinson's Superstitions – at www.channel4.com

Why people believe in superstitions – at www.psychmechanics.com

Dewey Decimal

130

Memory

53 List the Lists

Children with dyslexia very often have difficulty with memory. This can be a problem with short-term working memory – that is, holding two or more pieces of information at the same time and carrying out an activity simultaneously. It might also be a problem with long-term memory, and much of that is due to difficulty in organising the material at the time of learning. Information will be retained much more easily and more effectively if it is organised and arranged in a logical way to make recall easier.

The aim of this activity is to help children to organise materials and arrange the new material into lists and categories, as an aid to memory and recall.

Requirements

- pens or pencils
- lined paper

Vocabulary

Verb: categorise

Adjective: organised

Noun: inventory

Associated Words

Word	Meaning and example
recap	
checklist	
elaborate	
priority	
category	

Main Activity

Part 1

Children should work in small groups. Each group has to select a theme (e.g. sport, hobbies, shopping, pocket money). They then have to make priority lists for their selected themes. An example of 'shopping for the kitchen' could include:

- laundry powder
- dish cloth
- new mugs
- milk
- yogurt.

Each group should have 20 items for each list and then put them in priority order and number them accordingly. To make this task more demanding, you could introduce a timer so that the children get three minutes to make up their list. At the end of that time, see which group has the most items. All of the items must be appropriate and relevant.

Part 2

Each group now gets three minutes to remember their lists; at the end of that time, the list is taken from them. Next, the whole group listens in silence to music for three minutes. They then have three minutes to practise among themselves, and write down the items they remember, and try to put them in priority order. They then recite them to the rest of the group in order.

Teams get one point for each item remembered, but they lose a point for each item that is out of order. They may end up with a negative score! Try to make it a fun activity.

Optional Activity

Ask the group to put their list into a visual format. They do not need to do actual drawings but can use icons or letters made visually appealing.

Red Herring

Organisation can hold the key to a good memory. Practice at organising can therefore be useful. Ask the children in groups to organise an outing to the local zoo – they need to consider all the main points, and take into account safety, punctuality, accessibility, educational value, etc.

Websites

15 memory tricks – at www.apartmenttherapy.com

Memory techniques – at www.oxford-royale.co.uk

Dewey Decimal

150, 153

54 Kim's Game

Games can be fun and exciting – and we know that fun activities are the best way for many children to learn. This is important for children with dyslexia as they can find it difficult to remember information, particularly lists; if they find something challenging, then that activity is likely to be avoided. Yet practice at memorising information can strengthen memory. The aim of Kim's game is to strengthen memory through practice, and as it is in the form of a fun activity it will be welcomed and enjoyed by children.

The aim of the activity is to strengthen memory, using a variety of objects in a multi-sensory way. This activity can also help the child to appreciate the value of grouping items by association. By chunking items together, they learn that this strategy can support recall and retention. It can also be a good warm-up prior to a main lesson.

Requirements

- a wide range of 10–20 small objects, to fit on a tray (including objects from similar categories – e.g. stationery – and some unusual objects)
- a tray or similar
- something to cover the objects
- a timer

Vocabulary

Verbs: memorise, group

Adjectives: scary, rough

Nouns: mask, stapler

Associated Words

Word	Meaning and example
noun	
memory	
speed	
recall	
association	
remember	
grouping	

Main Activity

It is a good idea to enable the child to use themes or categories to help in remembering the items, so you might want to bear this in mind when selecting the objects. For example, you could include a group of stationery items such as a ruler, stapler, paperclip and scissors.

Place objects randomly (separate items from similar categories) on a tray. Allow children around 90 seconds to memorise the objects. Encourage the child to touch the objects, as this may also help to strengthen the memory trace. Engage the child in a conversation about all the objects and discuss, for example, colours and any objects that might have a smell (e.g. a tin of mints). This will help to encourage the use of all the senses. Build up the number of objects gradually to 21, then 24. For an optional variation on this activity, remove items and ask the children which have been taken away.

The words in the table above can be discussed in the context of the activity.

Optional Activity

Children can record the items on the tray using their mobile device, and practise listening to their own voice while looking at the objects. They should then cover the objects and see if there is an improvement in their recall.

Red Herring

Look at the history of memory. For example, how did the Romans remember things? You can Google this.

Dewey Decimal

150, 153

55 Picture Card Prompts

Any activity that can help to develop focusing, attention and memory is worthwhile for children with dyslexia. Visual activities can also be beneficial, as they are more likely to engage with visual activities than with text.

The aim of this activity is to develop focusing and attention to detail and provide supportive practice at developing memory skills.

Requirements

- a collection of images

Vocabulary

Verb: recall

Adjective: amazing

Noun: novel

Associated Words

Word	Meaning and example
image	
content	
colour	
scene	

story	
annotate	
graphic novel	

Main Activity

From your collection of various images, place ten on a wall for display. You should number these. The images can be art pictures, media photos or magazine portrayals. Old calendars are a great source for images – and a good way to recycle out-of-date calendars!

Select a picture, and discuss with the children any characters, objects, colours, scenes and the general content. Introduce the word 'annotation' and discuss this term with them. Demonstrate this process a number of times. You then ask children to make notes about the image you selected while you are discussing it with them.

After this warm-up, give each child the number of one of the displayed pictures. Set a timer for three minutes, and at the end of this time children should return to their work areas. The images they studied should be behind them (or covered if this is not possible). They should then list as many things as they can remember about their allocated picture.

Offer children the option of drawing/sketching the image from memory, if this is easier for them. Allow around five to ten minutes for this part of the activity. On completion of this stage, they can return to the images on the wall and check how well they did!

In turn, ask the children to describe their pictures while looking at the image. Discuss with them how this might help recall. A further option is to carry out this activity in pairs, and see if teamwork and combining strengths are helpful.

Optional Activity

Select from your image collection pictures with people in them. Photocopy enough for the activity and distribute these to each child. Ask the children to create some dialogue from the images. Use bubble speech to make it easier for them. This part of the activity can be associated with the popular programme called *Visualizing and Verbalizing for Language Comprehension and Thinking* by Nancy Bell.

Red Herring

Take one image from your collection and focus on location, time and what is happening. Use this activity as a means to discuss various aspects about the image content – for example, a picture of a ship could develop into a conversation on pirates, Vikings, luxury cruises and disasters (e.g. *Titanic*, *Costa Concordia*).

Tip

When the opportunity arises, collect images from magazines, tabloids, art gallery cards and marketing dispensers (train stations and airports). A variety of diverse and thought-provoking images are a great resource for this activity. Many of these images are free. Build up a good collection for choice and variety.

Websites

Visualizing and Verbalizing program – at https://lindamoodbell.com

Costa Concordia disaster – at https://en.wikipedia.org

Annotating text examples – at www.pinterest.com

Dewey Decimal

750, 770

56 Pelmanism

Children can improve their memory through the kinaesthetic experiences of actually doing a task. This can be very effective if carried out in a fun way and through games.

The aim of this activity is to improve memory and focus, through the activity below which involves matching pairs using playing cards.

Requirements

- packs of cards

Vocabulary

Verb: deal

Adjective: careful

Noun: cards

Associated Words

Word	Meaning and example
concentration	
matching	
attention	
memory	
shuffling	
anagram	

Main Activity

'Pelmanism' takes its name from Christopher Louis Pelman. It is a card game that involves matching pairs – two kings, two aces, two cards of the same number or, for younger children, two cards of the same suit.

The full pack is laid face down, and spread out over a large surface, preferably a table that allows all the children to see the cards as they are turned over. The first player turns over any two cards, leaving them visible for the other players to memorise, unless they are both the same – in which case, the successful player removes these cards from play and keeps them. If unsuccessful, the cards are turned back over in their same position on the table. It is important that everyone sees the cards clearly, and that they are placed back in exactly the same position so that spatial memory can be effective.

Play continues until all the cards have been removed. Players count up the cards they have and divide them by two to determine how many pairs they have collected. This involves a little bit of mental numeracy. The winner is the child who has collected most pairs.

If there are as many as six to eight children, there is the option to have two groups playing. This can provide a bit of fun and mild competition to finish first. Children can decide if they would like to play using this option.

Between games, children should take turns at shuffling the pack. This helps each child with dexterity.

Optional Activity

Pelmanism was a system of training the mind which was popular in the UK during the first half of the 20th century. Note that the 20th century refers to the 1900s. Discuss this with the group and run through the centuries with some questions. For example:

- In which century was the French Revolution? (18th)
- In which century was the First World War? (20th)
- In which century was the Battle of Hastings? (11th)

Children can search the internet for some interesting facts from each of these centuries. This could be followed by a discussion and comparison of facts. This develops the skills of talking and listening, and group work. You could vary the centuries for future sessions.

Red Herring

This follows from the discussion of the rules of Pelmanism. Can you make another word from the letters in the word 'rule'? (Answer: lure.) What does it mean? (A decoy, to entice, to lead astray from one course. For example, a spider could lure a fly into its web.)

An anagram is a word or phrase formed by rearranging the letters of a different word or phrase, typically using all the original letters exactly once. The following example can be used to demonstrate:

LISTEN – SILENT

BAT – TAB

RAT – TAR

Children can make up or look up some anagrams, and take turns to display their words for code-cracking.

Websites

Anagram solver – at www.wordplays.com and www.wordfinders.com

Solve your anagrams – at www.thewordfinder.com

Pelmanism – at https://en.wikipedia.org

Dewey Decimal

790

57 The Kluge

Memory games are always fun for children; if played in teams, this can be more fun as those with less good memories can still participate quite actively.

The aim of this activity is to improve memory by focusing on an audio-visual video clip that shows memorable feats of skill and daring. It is a team-building activity with useful follow-up activities.

Requirements

- a computer and access to the internet
- a list of prompt questions (provided below)

For optional activities, you will need:

- a golf putter
- golf ball
- corks
- playing cards
- a bucket
- juggling balls
- access to the FreeRice app

Vocabulary

Verb: prompt

Adjective: complicated

Noun: contraption

Associated Words

Word	Meaning and example
skill	
daring	
memorable	

precarious	
incredible	
ingenuity	
implausible	
contrivance	

Main Activity

Read the prompt question sheet (the list is provided below), then turn it over so that the children cannot refer back to it. Then get them to watch the film clip Red Bull Kluge from YouTube. Hold on to your seat!

The following prompt list can be adapted or extended to suit your requirements (e.g. ten Red Bull questions for the first three minutes of the video clip):

1. Who jumps out of the helicopter?

2. What is the first sporting activity that Joey is doing?

3. What colour is Joey's T-shirt?

4. What does Joey trigger?

5. What sport is Robbie playing next?

6. What machine cuts the wooden framework?

7. Can you remember the first name of the cyclist?

8. How many light bulbs were broken by the ball?

9. After the BMX bike stunts, what colours are the flags?

10. What is the red number on the blue rally car?

Kluge answers:

1. Sean McCormack

2. Skateboarding

3. Yellow

4. Wooden model motorbike

5. Golf

6. Chainsaw

7. Danny

8. Four

9. Green, yellow and red

10. One

After watching the video, children should complete as many of the questions as possible on the back of the prompt question sheet. Then discuss this as a group.

Watch the clip again, check answers and discuss with the children how they used their strategies to remember these activities and actions.

Kluge is a German word meaning computer slang for soft-hard configuration. The Kluge video shows a Heath Robinson style of structure, which follows a sequence of events. It appears to be chaotic, but achieves an end result, with many individuals contributing a high level of skill in their discipline, to complete the activity. They face challenges, but overcome them using confidence in their strengths, skills and abilities. This could be seen as a way of viewing challenges faced by some people who have SpLDs, and how they overcome them. As facilitators, we can help by using a variety of strategies and supporting children through the process of how they learn to learn and engage. Confidence is key.

Optional Activity

Create a mini-Kluge in a space suitable for setting up a sequential activity. As a child completes an activity, this triggers the next one.

The following sequence for this activity should not be extreme:

1. Children (say four or five) are set up in position.

2. First child tries to throw three playing cards into a bucket at a distance of one metre (three feet).

3. Second child putts a golf ball into a target.

4. Third child drops two corks until two are balanced on their ends (see 'Spelling Corks' activity, Section 2, Part 1, for more information).

5. Fourth child plays the synonyms game from the English grammar section of FreeRice, with a target of 50 grains of rice.

6. Fifth child and first child have a ping-pong rally, spelling 'K l u g e' (see 'Spelling Ping-Pong' activity, Section 2, Part 1).

7. Finish.

Depending on the number of children in your group, you may have to get children to do two activities, or you might need to reduce the activity triggers. This part of the activity can be adapted to suit the group.

Red Herring

Read extracts about William Heath Robinson by using websites such as Wikipedia.

Children can then research more information about Heath Robinson. They should make a list of some of the key words relating to Heath Robinson, and prepare a discussion about his life, his achievements and legacy to present to the group.

Tip

Danny MacAskill is an extraordinary stunt cyclist. You can watch a seven-minute video clip on YouTube for sheer enjoyment and discussion.

Websites

Red Bull Kluge – at www.youtube.com

Heath Robinson – at www.heathrobinsonmuseum.org

Danny MacAskill, stunt cyclist – at www.youtube.com

Dewey Decimal

530, 600, 790

58 Smells

A number of factors contribute to what we call a 'good memory'. One of these is practice – practise using your memory and being aware of the prompts and cues that can jolt your memory.

The aim of this activity is for the child to become aware of smell as a tool for practising using memory and developing effective memory skills. The focus of the activity is the sense of smell, and how to use this through an experiential activity. The child should become aware of how smell can help with memory and recall.

The sense of smell is closely linked with memory, probably more so than any of our other senses. Those with full olfactory function may be able to think of smells that evoke particular memories – the scent of an orchard in blossom conjuring up recollections of a childhood picnic, the smell of cut grass and a sporting activity, the smell of candy floss and funfairs or circuses.

Ask the children if they can think of any strong memories triggered by smells.

Requirements

- a list of ten smell examples (e.g. banana, apple, rubber, herbs, coconut, lemon, lime, washing-up liquid)
- text for reading and discussion (see below)

Vocabulary

Verb: smell

Adjective: wonderful

Noun: stink

Associated Words

Word	Meaning and example
scent	
fragrance	
aroma	
pungent	
acute	
lingering	
glomerulus	
odour	

Main Activity

We've got categories to describe our perceptions of taste, colours and sounds, but things are more confused when it comes to our sense of smell. A team of researchers have proposed a list of ten basic smells.

Ask the children to make a definitive list, along the lines of the example below:

- fragrant (e.g. florals and perfumes)

- fruity (all non-citrus fruits)

- citrus (e.g. lemon, lime, orange)

- woody and resinous (e.g. pine or freshly cut grass)

- chemical (e.g. ammonia, bleach)

- sweet (e.g. chocolate, vanilla, caramel)

- toasted and nutty (e.g. popcorn, peanut butter, almonds)

- pungent (e.g. blue cheese, cigar smoke)

- decayed (e.g. rotting meat, sour milk)

- minty (e.g. peppermint, eucalyptus)

They can use the internet to help them.

Optional Activity

Ask the children to write or type a paragraph of 50–60 words to describe the following:

- a sickening smell

- a warning smell

- an appetising smell

- a healthy smell

- a happy/emotive smell.

Factual descriptions can be followed by some creative sentences using each of the prompts. This develops creative writing.

Red Herring

Children could research into and discuss different dog types and their capacity for smell – professional sniffer dogs, and dogs used in work/safety – for example, police, army, rescue, security, health (cancer detection). They can use the internet to help them.

Tip

Gather a variety of prompts and keep them in jam jars for using during learning. Also, ask the children to find some samples to use for identifying.

Discuss the relationship between eating and smelling. How are taste and smell important in order for us to experience food and drink? Trial some examples – sweet and savoury.

Smell and taste belong to our chemical sensing system (chemosensation). The complicated process of smelling and tasting begins when molecules released by the substances around us stimulate special nerve cells in the nose, mouth, or throat.

Source: from www.entnet.org

There can be a lot of humour attached to some smells – ask the children to provide examples of this.

Websites

Ten basic smells – at https://io9.gizmodo.com

Dogs' dazzling sense of smell – at www.pbs.org

The sense of smell – at www.fifthsense.org.uk

How the sense of smell affects taste – at www.discoveryexpresskids.com

Dewey Decimal

150, 570

Part 3

Cross-Curricular

Introduction

The ability to transfer learning from one area of the curriculum to another is crucial for both a fuller understanding and for the development of concepts. Quite often, children with dyslexia can have difficulty with these factors. This means that each time they work on an activity, they see it as a new activity and may not realise that they can use the skills and the experience of previous learning.

We have attempted to highlight the importance of transferring learning in this book, and the section in this part of the book on different curricular areas can be an appropriate vehicle for this. We have included activities that relate to almost every area of the curriculum and have actively encouraged the transfer of learning across the curriculum.

We have also focused more specifically on certain areas such as maths (number work) and technology. These areas are important, but they can present a specific challenge for children with dyslexia. Children with dyslexia can have difficulties with maths because of the reading element. For example, they find it hard to understand a worded problem, or they might misread maths symbols and carry out the wrong sum. In addition, dyslexic children often have an underlying cognitive profile that can cause difficulties. Often there is a weakness in working memory and/or processing speed. This can have an impact on that child's ability to remember things such as number facts, all of the steps that are needed in a calculation, or the order in which steps need to be carried out. Some children might have a weakness in visual perception skills, and this can make it hard to interpret information that is presented visually – for example, in charts, graphs or tables. The activities in the number work section are designed to help support children in these areas.

We have included a section on technology, because children with dyslexia benefit from multi-sensory, active teaching and learning. Technological advances have made it much more possible to adapt learning to achieve this aim. The range of options is extensive, but this can be daunting to implement. The activities in this section are based on recommendations from teachers working in a range of contexts, and include animation activities and a review of apps, as well as specific programs such as 'Book Create' and 'Inspiration'.

Although much of the audience for this book will be teachers and others who work at a school, we are aware that parents will also wish to be involved in their child's learning activities or may even be home schooling or using home tutors. Most of the activities in the whole book can be used or followed up at home. We have also included a section of activities on 'home and school'. These activities were created so that the link between home and school can occur and develop. Essentially, all the activities can perform that function and this is an important ingredient of this book.

Dealing with dyslexia is not the responsibility of one person, and it should be seen from a wider perspective. Although there are increasing numbers of specialist teachers of children with dyslexia – and this is excellent and desirable – much of the responsibility for the day-to-day practice still rests with a class teacher or parent. We appreciate this, and have made the activities flexible so they can be used at different levels and for different age ranges.

The activities in this part will be beneficial to all and will reach out to those who may not be familiar with dyslexia and its ramifications. We also hope the recipients of the activities – children with dyslexia – learn to appreciate their skills and abilities, and, above all, their potential.

Number Work

People with dyslexia can have difficulties with maths because of the reading element. For example, they find it hard to understand a worded problem, or they might misread maths symbols and carry out the wrong sum. In addition, dyslexic children often have an underlying cognitive profile that can cause difficulties. Often there is a weakness in working memory and/or processing speed. This can have an impact on that child's ability to remember things such as number facts, all of the steps that are needed in a calculation, or the order in which steps need to be carried out. Some children might have a weakness in visual perception skills, and this can make it hard to interpret information that is presented visually – for example, in charts, graphs or tables. We have incorporated this in the maths activities in this section.

59 Ellipse

For a number of reasons, maths can be a real hurdle for children with dyslexia. Maths involves recognition of shapes and particularly learning the name associated with the shape. Maths also involves a great deal of mental processing and this can place a strain on working memory.

The aim of this activity is to introduce and reinforce the term and function of an ellipse. We are selecting ellipses because we find that familiarity with ellipses can help with structure and therefore support the child when using geometric shapes in maths.

Requirements

- A3 paper for drawing

Vocabulary

Verb: draw

Adjective: oval

Noun: egg

Associated Words

Word	Meaning and example
ellipse stage	
circle	
plane	
curve	

Main Activity

Start this activity by providing a definition of ellipse – for example, 'a shape that resembles a flattened circle.'

Introduce and model an ellipse on a whiteboard by tracing round and round a curved line. At this time, emphasise that children should use a light and relaxed grip. Demonstrate this using each hand alternately.

Next, ask the children to draw as many ellipses as they can, using the dominant hand. This activity is to help warm up and use the whole brain. The association of using and repeating the word 'ellipse' and of drawing it can help with long-term memory.

Repeat the exercise, using the other hand. Fill an A3 piece of paper in the manner of the illustration below. Use a light, relaxed action.

Now demonstrate the steps for drawing a cup, saucer and spoon. The steps are illustrated below.

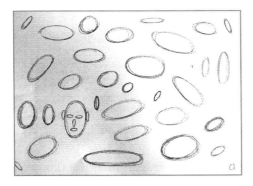 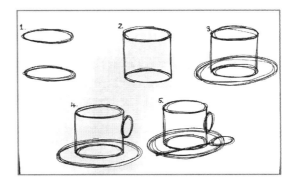

Optional Activity

Issue the children with plastic beakers. Ask them to hold the beaker vertically at eye level with the top of the beaker in line with their eyes. Next, ask them very gradually to angle the beaker towards their line of vision. Notice how the straight edge of the top of the beaker goes through a range of ellipses, until it becomes a full circle. They can continue after 90 degrees (there is an opportunity here to discuss this angle) in a downward direction, and see how the ellipses continue. The downward movement is slightly restrictive, but the effect can be seen.

Red Herring

Rugby Balls and American Footballs

Discuss how an oval ball bounces unpredictably. This can introduce terms such as 'anticipation', 'awkward', 'tricky', 'guessing' and 'judging' to reinforce language development. Outside, preferably in a field, playground or sports hall/gym, children can practise in pairs, throwing or kicking to each other and allowing the ball to bounce, rather than catching it. They should try to retrieve the ball as quickly as possible once it lands. This is also a good exercise for focusing and concentration.

Websites

Play = Learning (book) – at https://books.google.co.uk

Ellipse definition – on study.com

Melvil Decimal system – at www.librarything.com

Dewey Decimal

513.21

60 Framing

Children often learn best through incidental learning – that is, they are utilising other skills while they are embarked on a primary task. For example, when going to the zoo they will be reading about the animals, etc. This type of incidental learning can be very useful in maths. Often, children who find maths challenging can become quite easily demotivated and switch off. But if they are engaged in a practical task, such as making something, they may be unaware they are using their maths skills.

The aim of this activity is for the children to carry out a practical activity such as measuring, marking and sawing with the purpose of making a picture frame. They will be working with 45-degree and 90-degree angles, and they will be able to do this more successfully in a practical task such as this than with a problem in their maths notebook.

Requirements

- a computer with access to the internet
- scrap wood/picture moulding
- a small saw with a strong brass or steel back (for precise work)
- a G-clamp
- a mitre box (with angles of 45 degrees and 90 degrees)
- glue (impact adhesive)
- newspapers or covering material (e.g. a PVC table cloth)

Vocabulary

Verb: saw

Adjective: decorative

Noun: frame

Associated Words

Word	Meaning and example
mitre	
saw (noun)	
glue	
join	
measure	
clamp	
bond	
precise	
bleed	

Main Activity

Start by watching a YouTube video on how to use a mitre box and saw for an introduction to the activity.

The children should then do the following:

1. Practise sawing pieces of scrap wood until they are confident in making both 90-degree cuts and 45-degree cuts.

2. Measure 8 inch/203mm on the framing wood, and mark with a pencil. Line the mark up on the mitre box, and saw through.

3. In order to make a complete frame, eight cuts need to be made. Each of these mitred cuts is at a 45-degree angle.

4. Glue two mitred sections together, and allow to bond/set; this makes a right-angled joint section. Repeat with the other two pieces. This can be done one after the other so both L-shaped sections are setting at the same time.

5. Finally, glue the two L-shaped sections together (using impact adhesive or equivalent).

Children will have created a square frame, and can use this for framing a suitably sized image.

Optional Activity

Children can create or produce any image/photograph/magazine cutting that they want to frame. Allow for the image to bleed into the frame. This means that there is no mount or border. Alternatively, depending on the size of the image, they can make up a mount or border to suit.

Red Herring

> In the US, a frame-up (frameup) or set-up is the act of framing someone, that is, providing false evidence or false testimony in order to falsely prove someone guilty of a crime. Sometimes, the person who is framing someone else is the actual perpetrator of the crime.
>
> Source: from https://en.wikipedia.org

Children could search the internet to find some famous examples of a person or people being framed.

Tip

Keep sawdust from sawing and mix with PVA adhesive to form a natural wood filler paste to make repairs in the framing activity. Store in a recycled jar.

Websites

How to use a mitre box and saw – at www.youtube.com

Frameup – at https://en.wikipedia.org

Dewey Decimal

340, 600

61 Visual Spatial

We have included this activity because visual spatial skills are useful for a number of subjects such as maths, technology, physics and sport. With some guidance, children with dyslexia can perform well in visual spatial tasks, but many have difficulties because this can be an abstract concept and does require some visual manipulation.

Spatial ability or visuo-spatial ability is the capacity to understand, reason and remember the spatial relations among objects or space. Visual-spatial abilities are used for everyday use from navigation, understanding or fixing equipment, understanding or estimating distance and measurement, and performing on a job. Spatial abilities are also important for success in fields such as sports, technical aptitude, mathematics, natural sciences, engineering, economic forecasting, meteorology, chemistry and physics. Not only do spatial abilities involve understanding the outside world, but they also involve processing outside information and reasoning with it through visual representation in the mind.

Source: from https://en.wikipedia.org

Requirements

- a pack of playing cards
- highlighters
- enlarged wall display of the full alphabet
- a clock face

Vocabulary

Verb: navigate

Adjective: everyday

Noun: equipment

Associated Words

Word	Meaning and example
organisation	
assembly	
reasoning	
planning	
calculating	
surveying	

Main Activity

Children can practise walking up and down stairs and, while walking, spell each letter of their word with a step per letter. If stairs are not available, children can walk with a letter per step. (See also the 'Spelling Golf' and 'Spelling Ping-Pong' activities in Section 2, Part 1.)

Start with sequential activities, which will vary depending on the age of the child. This could include sequencing the alphabet for younger children and making up a travel itinerary for those who are older. Work on a range of sequencing activities. For example, ask the children to describe some of the things they do regularly, and the order they do them in, such as their morning routine, Saturday routine, etc.

North/South/East/West

Take a map of the world – a wall map or globe would both work for this. A globe might be more challenging, and this can be good for older children. In groups, the children need to make up questions for another group on the location of some countries, in relation to other countries. They can use the compass points between the main points (e.g. north, north-west).

Left/Right

This can be a practical activity where children have to find objects around them, with clues such as 'far left of the desk'. Develop this further by using the language of sailing and introducing terms such as 'port' and 'starboard'.

It is also a good idea to introduce children to the use of compasses – even one compass between them would be useful – and other ways of finding directions such as by locating the sun (care should be used here; children should not look directly at the sun).

Optional Activity

Crossword puzzles help to develop language and spelling skills, and provide an opportunity to practise writing in restricted zones. Noughts and crosses is very popular and can be accessed very easily. Focus on sporting activities, targets and directions (e.g. goals, posts, bullseye, tracks, rallies, snooker table pockets, sequence of coloured balls) to strengthen skills in this area.

Red Herring

Arrange workshops and field trips to local shops, landmarks and attractions, and these can be used to check out directionality. Ask the children to find landmarks by giving them compass directions.

Tip

'Visual spatial relations' involve the ability to see the relationships between items positioned in space. If children reverse letters when writing them, this might mean that they are lacking in this perceptual skill. Exercises in laterality and directionality can support children who experience this challenge. Multi-sensory methods that help to reinforce and strengthen this area include tracing, sky writing, rhyming, highlighting in colours and playing 'I-Spy'.

Websites

12 activities for visual spatial intelligence – at www.parentingforbrain.com

Visual spatial relations – at www.eyecanlearn.com

Directionality skills – at https://ot.eku.edu

Map reading – at www.getoutwiththekids.co.uk

Directionality (left/right) – at www.pinterest.com

Dewey Decimal

710, 780, 790

62 Armchair Olympics

The aim of this activity is to use sporting events to develop and consolidate skills of ordering, basic probability and decimal place.

Requirements

- access to the internet so that you can show video clips on a large screen to all children
- maths manipulatives or calculators, if appropriate
- score sheets (an example is provided below)
- printout of scoring rules (provided below)
- paper for recording team cumulative totals for each event
- certificates/small prizes for gold, silver and bronze team winners

Vocabulary

Verbs: participate, compete, persevere

Adjective: inspirational

Nouns: decimal place, cumulative total

Associated Words

Word	Meaning and example
Olympic	
Paralympic	
athlete	
achievement	
honour	
perseverance	
sensational	
cumulative	

Main Activity

The overall task is to create a mini Armchair Olympics competition, using live video clips to determine scores.

Distribute a scoring table to each child. At the top, there should be space to record the child's name and lane number. The table should have four columns and enough rows to record the child's place in each event. For example:

Event	1st	2nd	3rd
Men's Snowboard Cross		X	
200m Backstroke			X
100m Sprint			
100m Backstroke			
Women's Snowboard Cross			

In this table, the child will note his or her results in five separate sports activities. They have been selected because they are relatively short and show a range of participants and sports, and if the children are allocated a number from 1 to 6 corresponding to the athletes' lane order, every child will get some points. If you prefer to look for video footage of activities that are particularly relevant to the children, you might want to take these same considerations into account.

First, the children are allocated numbers from 1 to 6. This could be done by throwing dice, by putting the numbers on folded paper to be selected from a box, or by letting the children choose their favourite number. It does not matter if more than one pupil has the same number. Once each child has a number, they are put into groups of 3–6.

The children are then shown the scoring rules (the allocated points can be rounded up if necessary):

- If the athlete in your lane number (or in the table shown on screen) comes in first, you get 15.5 points.
- If your athlete comes second, you get 12.75 points.
- If your athlete comes third, you get 11.75 points.

Each child should be given a table for keeping note of their individual scores in each of the five races.

At the end of each race, the team should calculate their cumulative total score on a separate table.

Certificates or small prizes could be provided for gold, silver and bronze winners.

YouTube video clips can be used. It is worth opening each clip in advance, and keeping these open in separate windows, so that you can choose where to start (for instance, you might want to skip the adverts, or a long lead-in to the actual race). Search YouTube for the following:

- Men's Snowboard Cross, Sochi 2014

- 200m Women's Backstroke Swimming, Rio 2016

- 100m Paralympic Women's Sprint, London 2012

- 100m Paralympic Men's Backstroke, London 2012

- Women's Snowboard Cross, Sochi 2014 (warning: the winner's name is given before it starts, so you might want to scroll past this)

Optional Activity

Mount Gariwang lies around an hour south of the region of Pyeongchang in South Korea. It was named after a 15th-century king whose own supply of ginseng was grown on the mountain. It has a dramatic view, but now the view has been obscured by changes that were made for the Olympic Games.

Children could read articles on this on the internet and provide arguments for and against the changes that were made. Was it worth it? Why do you think countries would go to such lengths to host the Olympic Games?

Red Herring

Ask the children: Can you imagine going through all of the training and work, then throw your medal away? In 1960, Cassius Clay (who later changed his name to Muhammad Ali) won the light heavyweight boxing Olympic gold medal in Rome. When he got back to the USA, he was refused service in a 'whites-only' restaurant. He flung his medal into the Ohio River in disgust.

Incidentally, Muhammad Ali was so scared of flying that he wore a parachute during his flight to the Rome Olympics.

Websites

The Olympic Games – www.olympic.org

The Paralympic Games – at www.paralympic.org

Dewey Decimal

796

63 City Trip

The aim of this activity is to use the task of planning a city trip to develop and consolidate skills of prioritising, planning, arithmetical calculation and working with timetables.

Requirements

- tourist information on an accessible city or sizeable town (this could be found online as part of the activity)
- calculators or maths manipulatives, if appropriate
- large-sized paper for mind-mapping, or access to a computer mind-mapping program
- squared paper to create a diary page that can be divided into hours
- prize ticket with printed instructions for task (noted below)

Vocabulary

Verbs: plan, calculate, price

Adjectives: possible, preferable

Nouns: timetable, schedule, costing

Associated Words

Word	Meaning and example
prioritise	
feasible	
schedule	
tourist attraction	
marketing	

Main Activity

The overall task is to plan a trip to or within a city.

First, distribute prize tickets, with the following text printed on them. Read the instructions aloud to make sure that children have fully taken in the content:

> You and your friends have won first prize in a competition. You can spend one full day in a city of your choice. Your travel, all activities and food will be paid for. To claim your prize, you need to send a plan of what you would like to do and how much it will cost.

Check for understanding of the question. Ask the children how long their trip should be, what will be included and what they need to do to claim their prize. There is no limit to the budget in this exercise.

In small groups (of 2–4 if possible), children should start by deciding which city they will visit and what type of activities interest them.

Once each group has a rough plan, ask them to prioritise the steps they will need to take, to see what is feasible. For example, they might want to look first at travel arrangements. Will they take a train or a bus? Are some trains or buses faster than others? They might need to know opening times, event times, how long an activity is likely to take, etc. How long will it take to get there from the station? If there are several activities, looking at the map, what would be the logical order to do them in? Where and when will they eat? As they are looking at this, they will also need to keep a note of the various costs. Finally, they have to present their plan, with a list of prices and the total cost, in a readable form so that they can claim their prize.

Optional Activity

Children should print two copies of the map of the main areas they will be visiting. The group splits into two, and each group has a copy of the map. They sit back to back. One group has the task of reading out directions to get from one point on the map to another (e.g. from the activity venue to a café). They can only use directional words – 'take the second street on the left', etc. – and not street names.

The other group marks the route in pencil, and the aim is to see if they get to their destination. They should then swap, so that both groups have the opportunity to give instructions.

Red Herring

James Bond's codename '007' was inspired by the author Ian Fleming's bus route from Canterbury to London. Ask the children to find out what they can about Ian Fleming. What is it about the Bond books and movies that makes them so popular?

Tip

Microsoft provides a number of templates that can be helpful in different types of planning and scheduling. See: https://templates.office.com.

Websites

Travel websites can provide ideas and recommendations for activities and transport links. These can be searched online using terms such as 'tourist advice [city name]' or 'travel from XX to YY'.

Dewey Decimal

910

64 Overseas Trip

This activity involves planning a short overseas trip and would work well as a follow-up to previous activities.

The aim is to use the task of planning an overseas trip to develop and consolidate the skills of prioritising, planning, arithmetical calculation and working with timetables. It also involves taking account of different time zones and currency exchange rates.

Requirements

- access to computers for internet searching
- calculators and/or maths manipulatives, if appropriate
- large-sized paper for mind-mapping, or access to a computer mind-mapping program
- squared paper to create a diary page that can be divided into hours
- printed instruction sheets for task (details below; you should decide the budget and enter this)

Vocabulary

Verbs: plan, prioritise, calculate, compare

Adjectives: feasible, possible, preferable, cost-effective

Nouns: timetable, schedule, price, exchange rate, Greenwich Mean Time, discount

Associated Words

Word	Meaning and example
budget	
time zone	
currency	
airport	
passport	
visa	

Main Activity

The overall task is to plan an overseas trip, within a limited budget.

First, distribute instruction sheets, with the following text printed on them. Read the instructions aloud too:

You have been asked to provide suggestions for a short (1 week) overseas trip for you and some of your friends. The maximum group is 10, plus two adults. You have a budget of [£xxx] per person. Your suggested plan should include costs for the following (food will come from a separate budget):

- destination

- travel arrangements (flights/ferries/trains with timetables and prices)

- accommodation costs

Each person can take £xxx in spending money. What is the currency in the destination country? Provide three different quotations for the rate of exchange for this amount of money.

Check for understanding of the question. Ask the children how long their trip should be, how many people (adults and children) will be going, what the budget per person is, and what costs they need to cover. What do they have to do about spending money?

In small groups, children should start by deciding the trip destination. What is the time zone in the destination country? They should then prioritise the steps they will need to take to find out the best option for getting there. Is it possible to get a direct flight? How long are flight times? Is the route covered by a budget airline? Is it cheaper to arrange the flights separately, or to book a return trip with the same airline? What kind of accommodation is available? Are there discounts for large groups? They will also need to keep a note of the various costs. Finally, they have to present their plan, with a list of prices and the total cost, in a readable form.

Optional Activity

Despite being a huge country, India insists on having one national time zone. The single time zone seems to have been originally introduced to make it easier to organise the train network across the whole country. India chose to be five and a half hours ahead of Greenwich Mean Time. If you are in Britain or India, you can quickly work out the time in the other country by turning the clock upside down. Draw a clock on a sheet of blank paper, and using a pencil to mark times, calculate what time it is in India. Check this by adding five and a half hours to the time. What time is it right now in India? What time will it be in India when it is 8.30am in Britain? What time will it be in Britain if it is 7.00pm in India?

Red Herring

There is small island called Market Fyr in the Baltic Sea, which is only 300 metres long by 80 metres wide. It is owned by Sweden and Finland, so this tiny island has two different time zones. Finland is one hour ahead of Sweden. Ask the children to find these countries on the map, and locate the island of Market Fyr. Ask them in groups to find out five interesting facts about each country, and then to share these with the rest of the group.

Tip

Microsoft provides a number of templates that can be helpful in different types of planning and scheduling. See: https://templates.office.com.

Websites

What is GMT? – at https://greenwichmeantime.com

Greenwich Mean Time – at https://en.wikipedia.org

There are a number of travel websites that can provide ideas and recommendations for activities, and for transport links. These can be searched online using terms such as 'cheapest flights from XX to YY'.

Dewey Decimal

910

65 Design a Den

The aim of this activity is to use the task of designing a den to develop and consolidate the skills of prioritising, planning, arithmetical calculation and working with measurements, angles and scale.

Requirements

- access to computers for internet searching
- calculators and/or maths manipulatives, if appropriate
- large-sized paper for mind-mapping
- squared paper to create a scaled plan
- printed instruction sheets for task (provided below)

Vocabulary

Verbs: plan, prioritise, calculate, measure

Adjectives: squared, cubed

Noun: architect

Associated Words

Word	Meaning and example
area	
scale	
angle	
dimension	
space-saving	

Main Activity

The overall task is to work in teams to create a den to your own specifications. You each have the same basic shell – a shed with a door and three windows.

The dimensions of the shed are:

Height – 205 cm at the front; 30 cm lower at the back

Width – 305 cm

Depth – 150 cm

Wall thickness – 1.2 cm

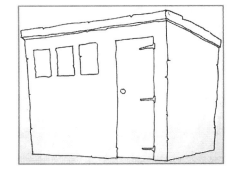

Distribute instruction sheets, with the following text printed on them. Read the instructions aloud:

> Your local hardware store is running a competition for the most practical and creative way to fit out a standard shed. You can decide what the purpose will be. In the past, winners have created a games room, a gym and a small cinema. You can design your own version in these categories or you can invent your own category. You need to provide a plan that shows what you would need to buy (or make) to put in the shed and where it would fit. You will need to take account of where the door and windows are, and the sloping roof. The plan should be made to scale.

Check for understanding of the task. Ask the children what categories they could enter, and how they have to present their competition entry.

In small groups, children should start by deciding the category/purpose of the shed. What steps will they need to take to create a plan of the inside of the shed? Where will they source the materials they need?

Optional Activity

Roald Dahl wrote his books in a small 1.8 x 2.1 m shed that he called his 'little nest'. Philip Pullman wrote *His Dark Materials* in a shed that he has passed on to another writer and illustrator (Ted Dewan) with the condition that it should only be used for creative purposes. Discuss the following with the children: Where would you prefer to work? Do you like peace and quiet and no distractions? Or do you prefer to have some background noise and activity?

Red Herring

In ancient Egyptian mythology, 'Shed' was a god of danger, deadly animals and illness. Ask the children to look this up on the internet. Do they know of any other ancient gods?

Tip

Search YouTube for tutorials that show how to draw a plan to scale and how to draw a floor plan in Excel.

Website

Shed of the Year – at www.theguardian.com

Dewey Decimal

729

Including English as an Additional Language (EAL)

Introduction

Although this section focuses on English as an additional language, it will be useful for all children in the group – particularly those with dyslexia.

In many ways, the challenges associated with dyslexia can be very similar to those experienced by EAL children. For example, difficulties associated with learning sound–symbol correspondence can be equally challenging for young children with dyslexia and for children whose first language is not English. Further on in age, the same applies to vocabulary development, grammar, punctuation and comprehension – particularly in the use of inferences. Both groups also need overlearning. That means they will take longer to achieve automaticity, and will need a lot more practice at doing the type of activities in this section.

It should also be recognised that some children whose first language is not English may also be dyslexic. This is an important consideration because it is believed that dyslexia is under-identified in the bilingual population. This would indicate that many bilingual students may have dyslexia, but remain undiagnosed because EAL (also referred to as ESL – English as a Second Language) is often mistakenly assumed to be the primary challenge.

The activities in this section will focus on the aspects above.

66 Adjective Wall

This activity will encourage EAL children to write, using a wider variety of adjectives. Often, children whose first language is not English write quite sparsely and they can be reluctant to use adjectives, or they may use the same ones repetitively.

The aim of this activity is to encourage the use of a variety of adjectives in writing, and particularly those adjectives that EAL children have not previously used or are not familiar with.

Requirements

- Post-It notes
- dictionary and/or access to internet links
- clear wall space

Vocabulary

Verb: scrutinise

Adjective: colourful

Noun: masterpiece

Associated Words

Word	Meaning and example
scan	
select	
variety	
novel	
decorative	
elaborate	

Main Activity

Children should refer to a dictionary and/or the internet for examples of adjectives.

First, each child selects four adjectives and writes these on separate Post-It notes. They then stick the notes on a wall. This will make a 'wall of adjectives'.

Next, each child selects four adjectives from the wall – not their own – and writes four sentences using each of the adjectives. They can work in pairs in this part of the activity, as some children may have difficulty in writing this on their own.

Children should then read out their sentences to others in their group. If there are four in the group, that would mean they have 16 sentences. The group then has to join all the sentences together, only using the following linking words – 'but', 'and', 'or', 'because', 'therefore' and 'however'. They should only use the same word a maximum of four times.

The group will then very likely have a hilarious story to read out to the other groups.

Optional Activity

Have an adjective competition. Each child selects the top three adjectives from the wall, writes them out and numbers them one to three. They should not use their own adjectives. All the selections are counted and tabulated, and an adjective rating table is developed. As an add-on activity, each group should then write a summary of their story in 30–50 words.

Red Herring

We have been creating an adjective wall. Ask the children to think of other famous walls in history – the Berlin Wall, the Great Wall of China, Hadrian's Wall, the Wall of Jericho, Wall Street and the Western Wall, Jerusalem. See the link 'Top Ten Origins: History's Great Walls' at: http://origins.osu.edu.

Children then select three walls and write adjectives to describe these walls. This can be done in groups. Once completed, these adjectives and the wall selected can be read to the whole group.

Websites

13 famous walls around the world – at www.huffingtonpost.ca

The world's most famous walls – at www.telegraph.co.uk

Adjectives – at www.gingersoftware.com

Examples of adjectives – at http://examples.yourdictionary.com

Using adjectives – at www.englishgrammar.org

Dewey Decimal

400

67 PT (Position and Time) Prepositions

One of the main challenges experienced by EAL children is developing written work. They may well have the ideas, and perhaps also the related vocabulary for the topic, but they often have difficulty in using prepositions and this can have an impact on their written work. They can easily either confuse words such as 'on', 'in' and 'at', or they might omit them altogether. They might also confuse words such as 'before' and 'after'.

The aim of this activity is to help children of all ages to learn and consolidate prepositions, and to achieve automaticity in their use. This is a whole-group activity that can be particularly useful for learners whose second language is English.

Requirements

- timers (one for every 4–6 children)
- paper
- prepared 'bingo' cards (example provided below)

Vocabulary

Verb: join

Adjective: long

Noun: stem

Associated Words

Word	Meaning and example
sentence stem	
position	
bingo	
appropriate	
between	
beneath	

Main Activity

Oxford Living Dictionaries describes prepositions in the following way:

> A preposition is a word such as *after*, *in*, *to*, *on*, and *with*. Prepositions are usually used in front of nouns or pronouns and they show the relationship between the noun or pronoun and other words in a sentence. They describe, for example: the position of something or the time when something happens.
>
> Source: from https://en.oxforddictionaries.com

These are the prepositions that will be focused on in this activity – position and time.

In preparation for this game, teach the children something about prepositions, or give some examples of position prepositions such as 'over', 'under', 'on', 'beneath', 'on top of' and 'between'.

Position Game

In groups of three, children select four objects. They can use any objects they have to hand such as a pencil, eraser and ruler. They are given five minutes, and during that time they have to place these objects beside another object around them and write a sentence describing this using an appropriate preposition. For example, 'The green pencil is underneath the table'. They must use different prepositions for each of the objects they have selected.

At the end of five minutes, each group teams up with another group. One group (group A) tells the other group (group B) their original four objects, and group B has to write appropriate sentences for each of the four objects. They are timed doing this.

Then they change tasks, and the first group (group A) has to write sentences (timed) based on group B's four objects. At the end, all the small groups indicate their times to the whole group, and a winning group is identified!

Then give examples of time prepositions – for example, 'before', 'at' and 'after'. Each group then has to make up sentences using these three prepositions.

Preposition Bingo

In this game, each group is given a bingo card. A blank example is shown below:

B	I	N	G	O

A variety of cards needs to be prepared in advance, each with a slightly different permutation of prepositions on it. This can be done by using a general template, and amending it slightly for each separate card.

The facilitator then reads out a sentence stem – for example, 'She left her pen _____ the table.' Each group has to insert the correct word. They can use a numbered page, and only need to put in the word next to the number. There are 20 spaces on the card, and the group that fills the 20 spaces shouts 'Bingo!'

Optional Activity

Each group makes up their own sentence stems (start with ten), with the preposition missing, and gives this to another group (and vice versa). At the end, they count up their total correct answers.

Red Herring

Find out about the origins of the word 'bingo'.

Using the internet, look at the history of the game as far back as the 1500s. Ask the children what it was called before it was known as bingo!

They can also look at its origins in the UK. Discuss this and ask the children why it has become popular in the UK.

Websites

Prepositions – at www.ego4u.com

What is a preposition? – at www.gingersoftware.com

Preposition list – at www.englishclub.com

List of English prepositions – at https://en.wikipedia.org

Prepositions with examples – at https://webapps.towson.edu

Dewey Decimal

400

68 Use My Name

As a follow-up activity from the one on adjectives, try this one which can be good practice at using adjectives and also a fun activity. It is important that children whose first language is not English have as much practice at using adjectives as possible. Ideally, this practice should be in a structured and meaningful format. For most of the activities in this section, the children are working in groups, and this is ideal for language learners as they may not have the confidence to come up with adjectives on their own, and may adopt a 'play safe' attitude.

Requirements

- paper
- pens and pencils
- computer and access to the internet (optional)

Vocabulary

Verb: recognise

Adjective: wonderful

Noun: person

Associated Words

Word	Meaning and example
define	
describe	
discuss	
gregarious	
intelligent	
thoughtful	

Main Activity

Working in pairs, each child writes their own name on a large sheet of paper – they need to leave space below for the activity words. They have to write an adjective for each letter in their name. If they have a short name, they can use a middle name (or invent one). The pair should discuss each of the letters and together decide on an adjective. They can make this into a work of art – colour it and pin it on the board. The group can then read all the adjectives from the board.

Each pair then has to select any four adjectives – not their own – write sentences with each of these, and indicate the meaning of each adjective.

Optional Activity

The pair selects two famous people – they can choose anyone they wish. They then do the same with these people, but try to write adjectives that can appropriately describe them. At the end, they read out *only* the adjectives to the group – they can give a clue such as movie star or football player – and the group has to guess who the person is just by using the adjectives as the main clues.

Red Herring

The Origins of Names

Look at the origins of the names of the people the children have selected and also their own names. What do their names mean? Where did they originate from? Why were they given these names?

Children can also search the websites of the famous people they have selected, and look for clues as to how they got their names and/or why they selected the names of their children. For example – David Beckham and his son Brooklyn.

See the following websites:

www.behindthename.com

www.ancestry.ca

Dewey Decimal

403

69 Verbs Charade

Language manipulation – being able to use parts of speech automatically in different contexts – is important for automaticity and language mastery. This applies to the use of verbs, as some verbs can confusing – for example, 'see', 'do', 'ask' and 'look' can be used inappropriately, particularly by those who do not have a great deal of experience in English. The aim of this activity is to reinforce the use of different verbs through actions, in order to reinforce when that verb can be used. Children with dyslexia learn more effectively if the task is multi-sensory and they are actively involved. This activity involves all the children and is fun, active and interactive.

Requirements

- picture cards (from magazines or hand drawn – e.g. an ear for the verb 'to listen')
- computer and access to the internet

Vocabulary

Verb: act

Adjective: funny

Noun: actor

Associated Words

Word	Meaning and example
mime	
pretend	
guess	
hilarious	
clue	

Main Activity

Arrange the children into groups of around six. Each child receives a different picture. They have to act out the picture until someone in the group responds with the correct verb. Once each child has had a turn at this, the group makes up their own picture from magazines or drawings, and one of the group presents this to the rest of the children. Time how long it takes the rest of the children to respond, and make a competition out of it.

Optional Activity

Ask one group of children to act out a scene from a play in mime form, and the other groups have to write down all the verbs that can be used in the scene. Ask the children to make up a daily verb chart, using some of the verbs they have noted in this activity.

Red Herring

Ask the children to find the definition of 'charade'. For example:

> Charade: a game in which the players are typically divided into two teams, members of which take turns at acting out in pantomime a word, phrase, title, etc., which the members of their own team must guess.

Source: from www.dictionary.com

On YouTube, children can watch a trailer of the 1963 movie *Charade*. Ask them why they think the movie was called *Charade*.

Websites

Definition of charade – at www.thefreedictionary.com and www.urbandictionary.com/define.php?term=charade

Verbs pave the way for language development – at www.hanen.org

Dewey Decimal

403

70 Who Am I?

Children can learn very effectively through games and fun activities. Additionally, games are usually multi-sensory and interactive, and these are two of the essential ingredients for teaching children with dyslexia. These aspects are also crucial in the teaching of second-language learners, and those whose first language is not English. It is important to use as many games and active tasks as possible. Children will engage better with such activities and will retain the information more effectively.

This activity is all about actions and make-believe play. It can harness children's imagination.

Requirements

- access to the internet for web searches

Vocabulary

Verb: construct

Adjective: extend

Noun: hobby

Associated Words

Word	Meaning and example
occupation	
action	
gesture	
posture	

Main Activity

This activity can work either individually or in pairs. It might be best in pairs if the children are not too confident in their use of English. Each pair looks at a list of occupations – see the following website for an alphabetical list of occupations: www.occupationsguide.cz.

Each pair selects around three occupations and mimes these to the group in around three minutes. Children are allowed to ask five questions only, and then they have to guess the occupation. The group then has to investigate the occupations that were not correctly identified, and make up appropriate questions for these that would make it easier to work out the occupation.

Optional Activity

Children can then do the same activity with hobbies, and select three hobbies appropriate to their age.

Red Herring

Children can go back to the list of occupations above. Each pair selects three unusual occupations that they are not familiar with. They should then research these occupations on the internet, and write a paragraph about them. They should then read their paragraph out to the group and the group can try to guess the occupation.

As an added task, they can again use the internet to work out the type of clothes that people would wear in different occupations, and the reason for that – smartness, safety, etc. They can also look at the qualifications needed for these professions.

Websites

Dave's ESL forums for students and teachers – at www.eslcafe.com

Interesting things for ESL students (word games, puzzles, quizzes, exercises, slang, proverbs and much more) – www.manythings.org

Merlot II: ESL learning materials – at www.merlot.org

WatchKnowLearn free educational videos for ESL – at www.watchknowlearn.org

Activities for ESL students (quizzes, tests, exercises and puzzles for learning English) – http://a4esl.org

Practise speaking English with a robot – at www.eslfast.com

Voice of America: learn American English – https://learningenglish.voanews.com

BBC resources for learning English – at www.bbc.co.uk

Aardvark's English Forum Resources for students and teachers of ESL – www.englishforum.com

Publication offering learners of English an opportunity to express and publish their ideas in English – www.topics-mag.com

A portal linking to all the British Council's websites for teachers and learners of English – http://learnenglish.britishcouncil.org

Bilingual dictionaries – at www.dicts.info

National Clearinghouse for English Language Acquisition – https://ncela.ed.gov

Dewey Decimal

408

71 Culture and Customs

It is important for children whose first language is not English to experience as much input in English as possible. However, it must be remembered that some children will still speak their first language at home, and that their home culture may well be immersed in their first language. For that reason, every opportunity should be made to use culture-appropriate activities in both assessment and teaching. It is also important for children from different cultures to share their culture and customs with others. This adds to the richness and diversity of the group, and provides an added and unique experience for monolingual children.

The aim of this activity is to provide all children in the group with the opportunity to talk about their cultures and customs. This will help to develop skills in oral language, and can also lead on to a written exercise. Children learn more effectively if they have a schema for the task. A schema refers to their own reference point, and the more familiar the topic, the easier it is for children to develop it in both oral and written form.

Requirements

The following could be provided, or added to, by the children:

- examples of traditional dress for different cultures – this can be a photo or, if available, the real thing!
- cultural artefacts – brooches, books, trinkets, etc.
- template of questions (shown below)

Vocabulary

Verb: adapt

Adjective: colourful

Noun: generation

Associated Words

Word	Meaning and example
annual	
religious	
culture	
custom	
traditional	
relation	
historical	

artefact	
stereotype	

Main Activity

For this activity, children should be in groups. Each group should have a mix of cultures. Each group decides on the culture they will explore. It is preferable that at least one of the children in the group should belong to that culture group if possible, although this is not essential.

Children should complete a structured template such as the one below, detailing the main points about that culture. This can be adapted and used in an age-appropriate way.

Culture Template

1. Origins of culture

2. Country of origin

3. Language spoken

4. Key historical events

5. Reasons for culture dispersal – i.e. why are the different cultures found in this country?

6. Religious customs of culture

7. Dress of culture

8. Pastimes and sports of the culture

9. Demographics of culture – try to get statistics

10. Famous personalities and people from the culture

Once the group has completed the template, they can present a talk to the others on that culture. It does not matter if the same culture is presented more than once – it is likely the responses will differ.

Optional Activity

If the children have any traditional dress, they should try to perform a short play acting out one of the ceremonies associated with that culture. They can still do this even without the benefit of traditional dress.

Red Herring

This activity can lead to values education – teaching tolerance and discussing conflict resolution at any level and culture. Search the internet for more information. See also the book *Multilingualism, Literacy and Dyslexia: Breaking Down Barriers for Educators*, 2nd edition (2016), by Lindsay Peer and Gavin Reid (Routledge).

Dewey Decimal

390, 391

72 Idioms

It is not surprising that children whose first language is not English tend to interpret statements literally – particularly when they are still acquiring mastery of English. This can also be an issue with children who are dyslexic. It is important therefore to devote some time to teaching idioms. This can be made into a game, and the use of visual images can help to make it multi-sensory.

The aim of this activity is to help children gain confidence in oral language, and understand statements that should not be taken literally.

Requirements

- a list of idioms (a website for this is provided below)
- drawing paper
- access to the internet for pupils to carry out web searches (optional)

Vocabulary

Verb: infer

Adjective: sliced

Noun: milk

Associated Words

Word	Meaning and example
spilt	
mustard	
lining	
grapevine	
grain	

Main Activity

For a list of idioms search the following website: www.smart-words.org
    Some examples of idioms:

Idiom	Meaning
to see eye to eye	
to sit on the fence	
a piece of cake	
a taste of your own medicine	
once in a blue moon	
on the ball	
to miss the boat	
to let the cat out of the bag	
to let sleeping dogs lie	
the last straw	

Make a list of idioms from the above website, and give four idioms to each group. You could put the meaning of the idiom next to it, but it is better if the group can discuss it themselves and try to find out what it might mean from the internet.

Each group has to make a drawing of each of their idioms. These are then presented to the rest of the children, who have to work out the message the idiom is giving. Try to give each group a different set of idioms.

Optional Activity

Ask each group to write a paragraph, or short story, using as many idioms as possible. Make this into a narrative to see which group can use the most idioms in their story.

Red Herring

Ask the children to search the internet to find out something about the origins of idioms.

One common idiom is 'to know the ropes'. This means that someone is experienced in what they are doing. This activity will help children to know the ropes as far as idioms are concerned!

> The origins of 'know the ropes' originates in the golden age of sailing, when understanding how to handle the ropes necessary to operate a ship and its sails was an essential maritime skill. By the mid-19th century it was a common slang expression, and it survives to this day.
>
> Source: from www.oxford-royale.co.uk

Find out about the 'golden age of sailing'. Why was it called the golden age?

Another common idiom is the one used throughout this book – 'red herring':

> Often used in the context of television detective shows, a red herring refers to something designed to distract or throw someone off a trail. So, a clue that appears vital to solving a mystery is often added to heighten suspense and may turn out to have been irrelevant; it was a red herring.
>
> Source: from www.oxford-royale.co.uk

A herring is a fish that is often smoked, a process that turns it red and gives it a strong smell. Because of their pungent aroma, smoked herrings were used to teach hunting hounds how to follow a trail, and they would be drawn across the path of a trail as a distraction that the dog must overcome.

Source: from www.oxford-royale.co.uk

Ask the group to give examples of red herrings, either from the activities they have done from the book, or any other examples – perhaps TV programmes or books they have read.

Websites

English idioms and their meanings – at www.oxford-royale.co.uk

25 startling origins of popular idioms – at https://list25.com

The origins of commonly used phrases – at www.rd.com

Dewey Decimal

400

73 Opposites

This is another activity that can be useful for EAL children, as well as children with dyslexia. It involves word meaning and word manipulation. Knowing the opposite of words indicates that the child will have sound understanding of that word, and the concept associated with the word.

The aim of this activity is to help the child to develop automaticity in the use of opposites. This can be helpful for comprehension and also for written work.

Requirements

- magazine pictures (optional)
- paper for drawing (optional)

Vocabulary

Verb: perform

Adjective: large

Noun: tree

Associated Words

Word	Meaning and example
opposite	
differ	
contrast	
extreme	
similar	

Main Activity

Ask the children, in groups, to write a list of items around them. They then use adjectives to describe each of the objects – such as colourful, large, exotic, grand and visual.

Each group then exchanges its list with another group, and the other group has to insert opposites for each of the adjectives. If they cannot find an exact opposite, they can insert one that might be close. The idea is that they understand the idea of differences and opposites. They may put this into two columns – one for vastly different and one for opposites.

Optional Activity

Hand out colourful pictures to the group – these could come from old magazines. The children describe the picture in opposite form (e.g. instead of 'a hot day' they can put 'a cold day'). They can also do a drawing that is the opposite of the picture given.

Red Herring

Try to find words that could be opposites but are not! For example, 'famous' and 'infamous' – make a list of these and show each of their meanings and why they are not opposites.

Opposite can be linked to the word 'opponents'. What is an opponent? Try to find some sports people/teams who are opponents – suggest why they are in opposition.

Search the internet to find the greatest rivalries in the history of sport. Choose two of these and say why they are rivals. Describe the rivalry between the opponents. The Fischer v Spassky chess rivalry in 1970–1972 is a good example. Ask the children to read about this and ask them to respond to the following:

- Why do you think this chess competition involved rivals?
- What is meant by the Cold War?
- Find out as much as you can about the origins and the development of the Cold War.

Also ask the children why they think in this case that sport was mixed in with politics.

Dewey Decimal

400

74 Diamante Poetry

This activity is a good follow-up from the previous activity 'Opposites' in this section.

The aim of this activity is to help children to use verbs, adjectives and nouns, and to use these in a 'diamante poem'. There is a seven-line sequence to this type of poem and it is very structured. It can be a fun activity, as well as helping children become more familiar with the use of grammar.

Requirements

- paper
- pens or pencils
- a computer with access to the internet (optional)

Vocabulary

Verb: describe

Adjective: poetic

Noun: sequence

Associated Words

Word	Meaning and example
diamante	
synonym	
diamond	
brainstorm	
descriptive	

Main Activity

Start with a definition of a diamante poem, then look at the sequence for this type of poem. Make a list numbered 1 to 7 of what each line represents. Information about this is on the internet.

The sequence for this type of poem is as follows:

- Line 1: beginning subject word
- Line 2: two 'describing words' about line 1
- Line 3: three 'doing words', ending with 'ing', about line 1
- Line 4: a short phrase about line 1, and a short phrase about line 7
- Line 5: three 'doing words' about line 7
- Line 6: two 'describing words' about line 7
- Line 7: ending subject word

There is a good example of a diamante poem called 'Lion' on this website: https://writeshop.com

Children should note that it is a diamond shape: it begins with the word 'Lion' and ends with the word 'Lamb'. A diamante poem must start and end with a noun.

Give the children the instructions and the examples above. Working in groups, they then try to make up a diamante poem. Give them a head start by providing them with some opposite words. This can follow on from the earlier activity on opposites.

Discuss with the children what brainstorming is, and allow time for brainstorming. During brainstorming, they should come up with some ideas for the topic, and as many descriptive words as they can think of. At this stage, the poem will not have taken shape, but they will have the materials (words). Once they have completed their poem, they can cut it out and paste it on to a blank sheet of paper, then decorate the paper.

Optional Activity

Children can add drawings to the poem. They may want to use drawings or pictures (cut out from magazines) instead of words.

Red Herring

Look at different kinds of poems – such as Shakespeare's sonnets. On the internet, you will find all 154 of Shakespeare's sonnets, together with analysis. Ask the children, in groups, to select several of these, rehearse them and then perform them to the whole group.

Dewey Decimal

400

Different Curricular Areas

75 What We Eat

Learning is often more effective when it is incidental learning and in a familiar context. It is even more effective when the learner has some ownership and responsibility for learning. Investigative activities are therefore ideal for children with dyslexia, as they can help to develop enquiry skills and finding out.

The aim of this activity is to encourage investigative skills and help the child make connections with the work they are engaged in across the curriculum. For example, this activity has an application in general science.

Requirements

- access to library or internet for research

Vocabulary

Verb: investigate

Adjective: sweet

Noun: cereal

Associated Words

Word	Meaning and example
harvest	
import	
export	
tariff	
ripe	
famine	

Main Activity

Ask the group to cut out the ingredients section of a cereal packet or cereal bar. They should then make up a list of six of the ingredients and complete a table, using the example below. They will need to use the internet or the school library – ideally, both. They can do this activity at any level – it can be tailored to young children or to those more senior. The details in the responses will be different but they can still carry out the task.

Ingredient	What is it?	Health benefits
flax		
molasses		
additive		
cinnamon		
colouring		
spelt		

Optional Activity

Ask the children to do the following:

1. Make up your ideal cereal bar/breakfast cereal. Decide what you would like to include and create an ingredients list.

2. Make a list of the health benefits.

3. Create an advert for the bar/cereal, highlighting its benefits. Who do you want the product to appeal to? Why? To help you with this, look at some similar adverts in newspapers or magazines or on the internet.

4. Make a list of the appealing points and how you will emphasise them – for example, a happy advert or a funny advert. Try to incorporate one of these themes into your advert.

Red Herring

Most memorable adverts have theme songs. Ask the children to discuss any theme songs that have made an impact on them. Ask them to try to make up a song to go with their advert.

Dewey Decimal

641

76 Dewey Decimal System

For many years, libraries have been a sanctuary for many children. A library contains a vast range of information and mysteries for the child to explore. Often, children take as long to choose a book as they would to actually read it! This is because libraries can be a place of excitement and curiosity. The internet and all the information that is now available at everyone's fingertips has minimised the key role played by libraries in the quest for knowledge. It is important that children do not lose out on this and that they learn and retain the skills needed to locate and access books in the library.

The universal system that has been developed for all libraries for cataloguing books is called the Dewey Decimal system. It is a universal classification system and it is important that children become aware of this system and familiar with its use and purpose.

The aim of this activity is to help the children to use the Dewey Decimal system effectively and efficiently. This can be useful throughout their younger years and beyond.

Requirements

- Dewey Decimal subject division sheets (print out copies – see website provided below)
- quiz worksheets (see below)

Vocabulary

Verb: look

Adjective: interesting

Noun: books

Associated Words

Word	Meaning and example
classification	
searching	
sequence	
demonstration	

Main Activity

Start by providing the children with information about the Dewey Decimal system.

The Dewey Decimal Classification

Conceived by Melvil Dewey in 1873 and first published in 1876.

It is a general knowledge organization tool that is continuously revised to keep pace with knowledge. The system is further extended through number building, interoperable translations, association with categorized content, and mappings to other subject schemes.

Source: from www.oclc.org

Discuss the Dewey Decimal system, using practical demonstrations from the library. Ask the children to locate book(s) on:

- computers (000)
- ghosts (130)
- mythology (290)
- drugs (360)
- dictionaries (420)
- volcanoes (550).

Have discussions and visit(s) to a library before asking the children to complete the quiz sheet below, by filling in the Dewey Decimal numbers in the spaces provided:

Worksheet

John was looking for his _____ theatre studies manual, to help him with his studies. Meanwhile Sarah, John's sister, was looking for a book about _____ fashion. As the day was coming to a close, the _____ sun was slowly disappearing behind the _____ hills. The _____ weather had been particularly nice for the _____ time of year. The kids were excited, because a circus was arriving in town the following day. The _____ circus was going to be setting up on the town moor next to the _____ river. John and Sarah hoped they would have enough money to visit the circus and would need to pay for a _____ bus as they lived on a _____ farm outside the _____ town. As a lucky omen, a flock of swallows swooped overhead and vanished behind the woods. Bedtime approached for Sarah and John, allowing them just enough time for a _____ snack.

Optional Activity

Using books signed out from the library, children read the 'blurb' on the back cover and make comments about the book using their own words – for example, what the book is about and specifying what the classification for this book is.

Note: to obtain all the information you need using this framework you may have to read further than the text above, but it is good practice to see how much information you can obtain from this text and how much easier it is to retain and recall the information.

Red Herring

Ask the children to watch *The Great British Bake-Off*, or equivalent regional programme. Relevant to this is Dewey Decimal 660 (Science and Technology). Find some books on how food is made.

Websites

Dewey Decimal system – at www.dewey.org/webdewey

Resources for the Dewey Decimal system – at www.pinterest.co.uk

Introduction to the Dewey Decimal system – at sixthformstudyskills.ncl.ac.uk

Worksheets for the Dewey Decimal system – at www.enchantedlearning.com

Detailed introduction to the Dewey Decimal system – at www.oclc.org

Dewey Decimal

001

77 Spinneracy

Children with dyslexia usually need support and guidance with study skills. They need support with identifying key aspects in text and also the different parts of speech. This activity can help with these and also with comprehension. It involves the use of spinner wheels. This is a transparent wheel, with an arrow spinner attached. It can be placed on top of a piece of paper with a picture of a circle that is divided into segments. A word or short phrase can be written in each segment according to the topic being discussed.

Requirements

- spinner wheels (example shown below)
- definition sheets (details provided below)
- glossary of terms

Vocabulary

Verb: spin

Adjective: rapid

Noun: glossary

Associated Words

Word	Meaning and example
hyperbole	
onomatopoeia	
connective	
pun	

Main Activity

Issue the children with spinner wheels and ask them to practise using them. Working regularly with spinner wheels will improve comprehension and speed of recall.

Make up a sheet of definitions, as in the example shown below.

Make up your own glossary of vocabulary wheels – or ask the children to build their own vocabulary wheels (these can be handwritten, or typed).

Definition Sheets

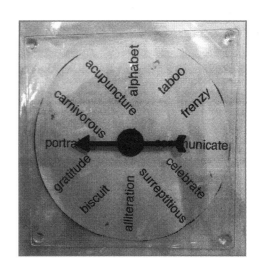

Make up lists of grammatical terms; the content will vary according to children's learning requirements. Use these sheets/ lists initially while practising with the spinner wheels. Develop children's memory by asking them to recall the meanings of the terms while using the spinner, without referring to the sheet. An example of terms that could be included is provided below:

- Verb – an action or doing word (e.g. 'James *ran* through the house, howling and shouting as he *went*').

- Adjective – a word that describes a noun; they provide information about the person, place or thing, such as its shape, size, age, colour or material (e.g. 'Jack Black, the *murderous* pirate, clung on to his *ancient*, *battered* cutlass').

- Noun – a naming word for a person, place or thing (e.g. 'The *sun* shone brightly on *Jennie*, who was sitting by the *shed* in the *garden*').

- Pun – a play on words (e.g. 'The racing greyhound had a bad case of fleas and *had to be scratched*').

- Alliteration – this describes the repetition of the same sound, letter or letters at the beginning of each word or most of the words in a sentence (e.g. the repetition of 's' in 'Squawking seagulls swoop on sunbathers').

- Simile – this is usually a phrase that contains 'as' or 'like' (e.g. 'John runs *as fast as* lightning'; 'She is *as innocent as* an angel'). Similes can be nonsensical and fun to develop.

- Connective – this is a word that joins one part of a text to another. Examples of connective words are 'however', 'because', 'therefore', 'while', 'also' and 'so'. If children can develop their use of connectives effectively, this will help to create longer sentences, and can improve the flow of writing.

Optional Activity

Taking verbs as the area to focus on, make up a wheel template for using with the spinner. Working in pairs, children take turns at spinning the wheel and creating a sentence using the verb selected. For example: 'falling' – 'The skydiver was falling so rapidly through the air, he didn't have a chance to link up with his friend.'

Red Herring

The red herring idea will now be very familiar to the child. Refresh what a red herring means (see the activity 'Idioms' in Section 10). Ask the children to develop their own red herring activities in groups. This can be made into a competition.

Tip

Make up a variety of spinning wheel words, themed for specific subject areas in all curriculum work. Use these for revision.

Dewey Decimal

400

78 Using the Whole Brain

This is a very important activity for young people with dyslexia. Often, they have the ability to solve problems, but may have difficulty in knowing how to do this. This can be because they are not accessing their whole brain – for example, if it is a language problem, they may try to solve it using language skills, yet it may be (for them at least) easier to solve if they used some visual images and 'problem solve' outside the box! To do this, they need practice at using both the language part of the brain and the visual hemisphere. They can also be encouraged to think in a random and not necessarily sequential way.

The aim of this activity is to strengthen the connections between the left and right hemisphere, and to encourage the child to use the whole brain. This activity can also be used as a warm-up exercise for a main activity. Also, using both hands equally benefits both sides of the brain.

Requirements

- A3 paper
- pencils

- sticky tape
- modelling clay

Vocabulary

Verb: fold

Adjective: continuous

Noun: brain

Associated Words

Word	Meaning and example
whole brain	
ambidextrous	
hemisphere	
simultaneous	
visual	

Main Activity

Instructions for the children:

1. Start by folding an A3 piece of paper, making a crease line down the middle, and then unfolding it again.

2. The paper should then be laid out flat, with the fold mark visible in the centre.

3. Fix the paper to the desk using the sticky tape.

4. Take a pencil in each hand, and starting at a centre point on the fold line, lightly draw a continuous line with each hand simultaneously.

5. Carry on with this until both hands meet at the same point – this should be somewhere along the fold line.

The result should be accurate mirror images either side of the fold line. Explain to the group that the whole brain has been engaged in carrying out this action.

Repeat this process a few times and create a variety of images.

Discuss the process and rationale behind it with the group. Also discuss the term 'automaticity', suggesting that skills can become automatic through practice.

Red Herring

For some exercises, ask the children to use their non-dominant hand. They can try this as an activity by using a plastic knife and fork to cut modelling clay, simulating food. In their daily routine, the children can use their non-dominant hand to brush their teeth. Discussion can follow to share the experience of these exercises.

Tip

Search the internet for information about the benefits of drinking water.

Websites

Easy-to-understand scientific information on brain health – www.hellobrain.eu

Brain games – at www.brain-games.co.uk

Dewey Decimal

100–199

79 Badge-Making

Young people with dyslexia need experience at working as part of a team. They need that sense of belonging and fitting in that can often be obtained by being a valued member of a team. This activity involves working and problem solving together. It involves badge-making, which is a very practical activity. Children with dyslexia usually enjoy this activity and can often take the lead because it can be well within their comfort zone.

The aim of the activity is to develop practice in using a sequence, which children with dyslexia can often find challenging. Once they know the sequence, the actual tasks and the process can be enjoyable and successful. This is essentially a team-building exercise. It involves designing the badge, assembling the parts, making the artwork and ensuring the finished product is correct according to the design.

Requirements

- badge-making machine
- templates
- 2 x G-clamps

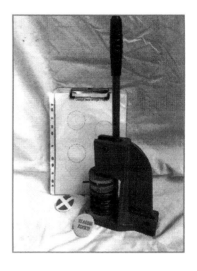

Vocabulary

Verb: clamp

Adjective: colourful

Noun: badge

Associated Words

Word	Meaning and example
create	
draw	
pressure	
design	
align	

Main Activity

We find this activity is excellent for sequencing, because the same procedure is followed over and over again. Mistakes may well be made, and this is a good learning experience because the experience will lead eventually to success.

First, demonstrate the complete process of making a badge. Begin by clamping the badge-making machine to a table or desk. Along with the badge-making machine, you will have a circular cutter, tin badge tops and badge seals.

Images can be obtained from magazines, newspapers, leaflets, flyers, etc. Alternatively, children can draw their own images or take photos using a mobile phone. You could take a small group of children out locally and encourage them to look for any interesting images or texts.

Badge-making can be linked to project work. It is ideal for charity fundraising, because many badges can be produced in a short time. Discuss with the children the charities to be supported. Badges can also be personalised to order.

Optional Activity

Create a 'word of the week' and use this word as the image on the badge. This reinforces the learning process and can make the word learning more memorable.

Red Herring

Think of your own Red Herring activity! Or ask the children to make one up.

Tip

There is a great range of reward badges available or you could make up your own for different types of achievement.

Website

Badge-making machine: how it works – at www.londonemblem.com

Dewey Decimal

690

80 Questioning Questions

One of the key learning aims for young people with dyslexia should be to help them become self-sufficient in learning, and therefore more confident and independent learners. Good questioning technique is important for that, because it can help with self-questioning. This in turn can provide a route to independent learning.

The aim of this activity is to develop good questioning techniques, and also to help the child to gain an understanding of different types of questions.

Requirements

- access to a computer
- a dictionary

Vocabulary

Verb: question

Adjective: effective

Noun: question

Associated Words

Word	Meaning and example
interrogate	
enquire	
inquest	
rhetorical	

Main Activity

Begin by indicating how important questions are for discussion; this leads to discussing the purpose of a question. Discuss how questions are used in everyday contexts. Think of all the people who may ask questions as part of their job – such as police officers, teachers and transport workers.

Essentially, a question is a linguistic expression used to make a request for information or the request made using such an expression. The information requested is provided in the form of an answer or response.

Questions have developed a range of uses that go beyond simply obtaining information from other people. Rhetorical questions, for example, are used to make a point; an answer is not expected – for example, 'Are you kidding me?', 'Is this supposed to be some kind of a joke?', 'Who cares?', 'Why bother?', 'How should I know?' Ask the children to think of some of their own.

Discuss the following: 'There is no such thing as a stupid question – or is there?'

Questions are used in a variety of settings. Ask the children to provide examples.

Task

Ask the children to make up an incident. An example of a bank robbery is provided below:

Late yesterday afternoon, just before (1) _____, a gang of robbers burst into the Leith Street branch of the Star Bank and stole approximately (2) £_____ along with items from security boxes. Eye witnesses saw (3) _____ characters enter the bank. They possessed weapons and wore balaclava masks over their faces.

When a security guard tried to (4) _____ the villains, they (5) _____ him. The guard is now (6) _____. The robbers then forced the customers and staff to lie on the floor while the robbery was taking place.

Police arrived on the scene rapidly, but so far have little information to work on. The robbers escaped in a (7) _____ which police later found abandoned in a terraced street about three miles from the bank.

The idea here is that one child, or group of children, has the full version of the text, and the other child or group of children will ask questions to find out the missing information. In order to do this, they should start by compiling a list of things they need to know. They could use the following as a guide:

1. When _____ ?

2. How much _____ ?

3. How many _____ ?

4. What _____ ?

5. What _____ ?

6. Where _____ ?

7. How _____ ?

Children could make up their own bank robbery story, with suitable questions.

Different Questions

Discuss with the children the different settings where questions are routinely asked; for example:

- In a court of law, defence and prosecution lawyers question witnesses to find out the truth of what happened.

- In an interview, the employer asks candidates a series of questions to find out if they are suitable for the job.

- In a hospital or clinic, the doctors and medical staff ask their patients about the background and symptoms of their illnesses or injuries.

- In an exam, students are provided with questions that aim to find out if they know and understand the subject. (Understanding the question is a key part of being able to answer effectively.)

- After a crime or accident, detectives and police question bystanders to establish what has happened.

- In class, teachers ask pupils questions to test their knowledge of subjects.

- Taxi drivers ask passengers where they want to go.

Optional Activity

Use a topical piece of text or a novel that children are working on. Ask the children to devise some questions and to take turns in asking and answering.

List some other situations where questions would be necessary and explain. For example:

- Tourist information office: 'What is the best way to get a ticket for the concert in town next week?'

- Restaurants and diners: 'Do you have a vegetarian option for this dish, and what are the ingredients?'

- Travel information, local and further afield: 'I would like to visit the seaside attractions, and was wondering how to get there?'

Find out how the word 'question' originated.

Red Herring

Think of your own Red Herring activity! Or ask the children to make one up.

Tip

Questions are used from the most elementary stage of learning to high-level research.

Website

The question mark – at https://en.wikipedia.org

Dewey Decimal

352.3

81 Sounds

This activity can be suitable for all ages – including young children. Awareness of sounds and different sounds is very important for developing reading and pre-reading skills. Children with reading difficulties often have difficulty in manipulating sounds, and this is an important skill for decoding and for reading. This activity gives children the opportunity to practise identifying different sounds in a fun activity.

It is important to encourage children with dyslexia to develop their listening skills. This can help them to extend their vocabulary and develop their concentration. Sometimes, listening does not come spontaneously, and children have to be trained and encouraged to listen.

The aim is to help the child to focus on using their sense of hearing to identify a variety of sounds. It can also help to develop effective listening skills and concentration.

Requirements

- sound clips (made up, or from a web source)

Vocabulary

Verb: listen

Adjective: deafening

Noun: ears

Associated Words

Word	Meaning and example
melodic	
rhythmical	
bang	
haunting	
clunk/clink	
buzz	

Main Activity

What is Sound, and Why is Sound so Important?

Sound is created when energy travels through the air and into the ear. There the brain interprets these energy waves as sounds.

Search YouTube for videos about sound and make a list of the different types of sounds you can think of. Engage the children in a discussion about how to hear sounds effectively.

Demonstrate three different sounds – for example, a door shutting, paper tearing, and using a stapler to join sheets together. Ask the children to describe these sounds. This is excellent for thinking about comparisons, and quite difficult. The activity supports attention and engagement.

Ask the children how we use sounds in sport – for example, in judging distance, communicating. What would happen if you eliminated sound in a game of squash or table tennis? Judgement is drastically affected. Discuss sound in music and how this ties in with emotions and feelings.

Optional Activity

This involves identifying sounds. Organise a quiz, using memory skills.

Provide a range of different sounds, and ask the children to recall all the sounds they heard. Some examples are shown below:

- knocking on a door
- car engine starting
- dog barking
- bird song
- vacuum cleaner
- clinking glasses
- frog croaking
- sucking liquid through a straw
- keyboard typing.

Ask the children to find an image for each of the sounds.

Red Herring

'Onomatopoeia' is a good word for practising spelling syllabically, and overlearning this grammatical device. Ask the children to break down the word:

On o mat o poe ia

(Pronounced: on-oh-mat-oh-pee-ya)

Roy Lichtenstein's art uses onomatopoeic terms, and his pictures are a great resource for exploring the effect of sounds demonstrated graphically – for example, 'Blam' and 'Varoom'. Collect images and use these to describe and discuss.

Discuss animals and the sounds they make. This is excellent for nature and related topics.

Discuss sound management for hearing safety at pop/rock concerts.

Discuss the use of earplugs/headphones for listening to music or when working in noisy environments.

Tip

Create sounds, and link them to images. Use recordings for rhythm work. Link spelling to the sounds that make up words. Make up some of your own Voice Memos using an app on a smartphone. Use the sounds for creative writing opening.

Websites

The 10 most addictive sounds in the world – at www.fastcompany.com

Sounds of life – at www.bbc.co.uk

Dewey Decimal

781

82 FreeRice

FreeRice is a non-profit website owned by the United Nations World Food Programme. FreeRice has two goals:

1. Provide education to everyone for free.

2. Help end world hunger, by providing rice to hungry people for free.

The aim of this activity is to support this programme and provide the opportunity for children to improve their knowledge of curricular subjects, using this fun application.

Requirements

- computer and access to the internet

Vocabulary

Verb: contribute

Adjective: admirable

Noun: volunteer

Associated Words

Word	Meaning and example
rice	
charity	
famine	
support	
giving	

Main Activity

Ask the children to read this text, or read it to them:

> FreeRice is an ad-supported, free-to-play website that allows players to donate to charities by playing multiple-choice quiz games. For every question the user answers correctly, 10 grains of rice are donated via the World Food Programme.
>
> Source: www.freerice.com

Subjects available on the FreeRice website include:

- English vocabulary (the original subject with which the game launched)
- multiplication tables
- pre-algebra
- chemical symbols (basic and intermediate)
- English grammar

- foreign language vocabulary for English speakers (French, German, Italian, Latin and Spanish)
- human anatomy
- geography (flags of the world, world capitals, country identification and world landmarks)
- the identification of famous artwork, literature, quotations
- world hunger.

A user's total score is displayed as a mound of rice and the number of grains.

Optional Activity

The children can produce a review of the FreeRice programme, with recommendations and comments. Some users posted comments to say that they found the adverts excessive and annoying, but that they appreciated that the adverts support the funding of the programme, so that it can be accessed free. Reviews can be posted with approval. Join the FreeRice community.

Red Herring

Discuss making fried rice as a meal. Find a recipe of it on the internet.

The discussion can develop in many ways – for example, experiences of eating out, good and bad; countries visited and the variety of local food presented; and staple diets in some of the poorer countries in the world.

Tip

Make up bags of rice (with number of grains counted) and use this as a quiz – can children guess how many grains there are in the bag? This can be done for fun and/or as a fundraiser. It is surprising how many grains are needed to make up a portion.

Websites

FreeRice website – www.freerice.com

Recipe for Chinese fried rice – at www.geniuskitchen.com

Dewey Decimal

381.4, 633.18

83 Annotation

Young people with dyslexia learn best if the material is presented in a multi-sensory manner. This could involve a visual, with some annotation below. It is important that all visuals are annotated because this reinforces the meaning of the picture and helps to consolidate and extend the child's vocabulary.

The aim of this activity is to introduce the term 'annotation', or, if the children are already familiar with it, reinforce the meaning of the term, through overlearning.

This can also develop habits for good practice that can support effective learning and more memorable and effective revision. This can in turn pave the way for independent learning.

Requirements

- face images (from magazines, newspapers, internet)

Vocabulary

Verb: annotate

Adjective: wrinkly

Noun: magazines

Associated Words

Word	Meaning and example
notes	
explanation	
recurrent	
specific	
points	

Main Activity

Start with a definition of the word 'annotation'. An example is shown below:

Annotation: a note added to a text, book, drawing, etc., as a comment or explanation: the act of adding notes or comments to something; the act of annotating something.

Source: from www.merriam-webster.com

For the warm-up activity, introduce and discuss the term 'annotation'.

Use an image of a face, which you can obtain from magazines, newspapers or the internet, and then add notes describing the features of the face – for example, smiley eyes, wrinkly forehead, thin lips, lank hair, small nose, crooked teeth, etc.

Next, develop a discussion on how we can annotate a newspaper article. It is best if you demonstrate using a headline, caption, image credit or part of the text. The annotation needs to be linked with the meaning or purpose of the text or picture.

Then ask the children to do their own annotation from pictures they have selected or from those that you have provided. Many cities have a free daily paper (e.g. *Metro*) which are a great resource, if available, for the purpose of using relevant material.

Then issue the children with an image (it can be interesting if you give the same one to all of them) and ask them to annotate the image fully. This helps them to focus on the whole picture. Discuss their responses. It is important to ask the children to explain their choice of annotation.

Optional Activity

Annotation Spelling

Ask the children to look at their annotation and to work out how many syllables are in the word 'annotation' (the answer is four syllables: an no ta tion).

Ask the children to make up cards and cut them into syllables that they can laminate. They can do this with the words in the annotations that they used for their own image too. The laminated cards can be used for revision.

Red Herring

Introduce the word 'nation' and ask the children to think of all the words that rhyme with nation. They can then discuss the meaning of 'nations' – for example, communities, identities, countries, sport (inter-nation-al) competitions. They can then look at the headlines from a recent international sport tournament (e.g. the Olympic Games) and note the headlines and the annotation when someone wins a medal.

Tip

The website www.theday.com is an excellent resource (subscription).

Websites

The Day (news website) – www.theday.com

Dewey Decimal system – at https://library.mtsu.edu

Dewey Decimal

370

84 Knots

Learning should be fun, but it also should have some useful purpose and one that the children can get some pride and a sense of achievement from. This activity has many different purposes, and it can have a useful goal for children.

The aim of this activity is to improve dexterity. The children will learn how to tie different knots for different purposes. This will help them to develop a useful life skill.

Requirements

- string or rope
- a computer and access to the internet for viewing YouTube or accessing websites

Vocabulary

Verb: tie

Adjective: difficult

Noun: knot

Associated Words

Word	Meaning and example
reef knot	
granny knot	

clove hitch	
butterfly knot	
figure-eight knot	
cow hitch	
fisherman knot	

Main Activity

Introduce the topic of knot-tying by showing YouTube clips of seven basic knots, to engage the children.

Discuss tying shoelaces and ties as everyday activities. Take an easy knot to begin with – for example, the reef knot – and practise this until the children are confident. They can work in pairs and support each other. Then progress to other knots. The key point here is overlearning, which is important for children with dyslexia; it can also help their memory skills.

Optional Activity

Find an extract on the internet about the procedure used by ancient mariners to estimate how fast their boat was travelling.

Get the children to note the other more recent methods of measuring speed. They should also consider what is meant by a nautical mile, and how this term originated. Ask the to make up a quiz for other groups on this subject. They can access the internet for help with this.

Red Herring

Introduce circus knots – this is a good avenue for branching off into the subject of circuses and can lead to an investigation of how circuses came about.

Tip

This activity was inspired by Patricia Spencer, who uses it with great success at Oak Hill School in Geneva. Tying and untying knots can be a great way to relax and wind down. For children needing time out for stress-busting, this is a real help. Tie a piece of rope from a door handle, and the child can tie and untie any kind of knot they choose.

Websites

Animated Knots – www.animatedknots.com

Knot – at https//en.wikipedia.org

Seven knots you need to know – at www.youtube.com

Why a ship's speed is measured in knots – at www.history.com

How to tie a scarf – at www.scarves.net

Dewey Decimal

514

85 Film

Ideally, effective learning should be as multi-sensory as possible. Film can be an excellent resource and a catalyst for other activities. Film can be used for information; it can also be a spin-off to extend learning and understanding of the topic.

The aim of this activity is to help the child to recognise the value of film, including on television, in videos and in present-day life. By giving children opportunities to study film, you are supporting literacy development, as well as an appreciation of related aspects and genres. Additionally, film can be exciting and dramatic, and it can engage the children in subjects that would otherwise be difficult.

Requirements

- access to a TV or computer with soundcard to show content to children and/ or access to the internet to show web content
- DVDs of films

Vocabulary

Verb: act

Adjective: dramatic

Noun: camera

Associated Words

Word	Meaning and example
actor	
prop	
lighting	
costume	
drama	
scene	
script	
director	
designer	

Main Activity

It is important to note how language changes depending on the genre. Choose a film to watch and break it down into sections for analysis, discussion and comments. Age-relevant films can be shown, and these can be based on curricular work – for example, *Of Mice and Men*, *Macbeth* and *To Kill a Mocking Bird*. Other films that we have found to work very well in stimulating wide-ranging discussions include *The Truman Show*, *The World's Fastest Indian* and *Touching the Void*. Ask the children to reflect on what aspects of the films are memorable and why.

Information Activity

Mitchell and Kenyon were Edwardian pioneer film-makers. They gave the general public the first opportunities to be filmed going about their daily lives, and as a result they are a useful source of social history. The films have been restored, so that the action is no longer jerky (because cameras were handheld), but is accurate in terms of movement. This makes the films seem more real to contemporary viewers. These fascinating, archive glimpses of times past will fully engage most children. Show some YouTube film clips, which you can find on the internet. Ask the children: What are your thoughts on looking at these videos? Do the people in the film look sad, happy or just puzzled? Why do you think this is?

Optional Activity

Bring some film reviews for discussion and/or ask the children to find some reviews of current mainstream films in magazines or newspapers. This also allows for a discussion with children of 'What is a critic?'

Red Herring

In cooking terms, a film is a thin coating or thin layer. Ask the children: What kind of food can have a film on it during cooking? This can lead on to a discussion of favourite recipes. Direct the children to cooking programmes (e.g. by Jamie Oliver).

Tip

A teaching guide to using film and television with children aged 3–11 is produced by the British Film Institute and available at: www.bfi.org.uk

A major intellectual aspect of the Primary and Early Years curriculum involves unpicking the construction of texts, fact or fiction, as well as understanding genre rules and seeing where artists and writers have transformed genres. This could include studying the representation of, say, a volcano (see 'Volcanoes' activity, Section 6, Part 2) in a documentary film for the subjects of science or geography.

Websites

Why study film? – at www.youtube.com

Teaching guide to using film and TV with children aged 3–11 – at www.bfi.org.uk

The Lost World of Mitchell and Kenyon – at www.youtube.com

Mitchell and Kenyon – at https://en.wikipedia.org

Dewey Decimal

600, 700

Creativity and Technology

86 Animation

The use of computers for learning is well established. Computer activities can also be fun and encourage creativity.

The aim of this activity is to look at how to use animation to support the learning process for children with dyslexia. This activity can, however, be useful for all children. It is also fun and can help children to develop memorable study techniques.

Requirements

- video recording device such as an iPad, smartphone or GoPro
- smartboard
- paper
- black marker pen

Vocabulary

Verb: show

Adjective: intricate

Noun: film

Associated Words

Word	Meaning and example
cartoon	
project (verb)	
character	
storyboard	
viewing	
technique	

Main Activity

Start by showing the children introductory YouTube videos on the subject. Find a video on eye drawing with open-and-shut effect that the children can copy.

Animation is a fascinating subject. Nowadays, most animation is constructed using computer-generated imagery. This can be abbreviated to CGI. Before this, animation had to be done by hand – all the objects and figures had to be hand-drawn, then photographed and transferred to film. This was a very time-consuming and difficult procedure.

How does animation work? The effect of animation comes from a rapid succession of sequential images that only minimally differ from each other. When you consider some of the cartoon films you have seen, you can only imagine the number of figure drawings that contribute to that film.

Apart from cartoons, animation is now used for special effects in movies and widely used in video games.

Use IMDB to highlight the most popular animation films. Look at other websites to see how animated movies are made and for comprehension.

Animation is an excellent way to present information – the children can do this to present a talk or start a discussion with the rest of the group. An animated presentation can hold the child's attention because it can use humour and visual stimuli, and can be a fast-moving information source. This can be excellent for the child with dyslexia. The internet can be a resource to help the children use animation in their presentations.

Red Herring

The Truman Show with Jim Carrey is a fascinating film to watch and can be used for extension work and discussion.

Tip

Building a storyboard from children's creative writing leads in nicely to working towards animation projects.

Websites

Benefits of using animation in the classroom – at www.fractuslearning.com

Educational animation – at https://en.wikipedia.org

Animation in education – at www.cgpundit.com

How to make stop motion animation – at www.youtube.com

Create awesome videos and presentations – www.powtoon.com

Dewey Decimal

777

87 Inspiration

Everyone needs to be inspired by someone or something, and this is especially important for young people with dyslexia. There are so many popular and accomplished individuals who have succeeded despite their dyslexia. Some in fact would say they have succeeded *because* of their dyslexia! Having to deal with dyslexia has made some people more determined to succeed, and there is also a viewpoint that being dyslexic can give you an extra edge in some tasks. Tom West, a prolific author who is also dyslexic, has given his most recent book on dyslexia the title *Seeing the Unseen*. He means that it is possible for people with dyslexia to use their imaginative powers to a level that many others cannot reach. In this book, West describes great feats in art, sport and technology achieved by people with dyslexia.

The aim of this activity is to help children with dyslexia to develop and harness their imaginative skills. The aim of this activity is to help them to understand the meaning of the word 'inspiration', and how to work out different ways of using their imagination and achieving the goal of 'inspiration.'

Requirements

- computer with access to the internet for web searches
- Post-It notes and A3 paper, or access to mind-mapping software (optional)
- computer with access to PowerPoint (optional)

Vocabulary

Verb: inspire

Adjective: unsuspecting

Noun: prosthetic

Associated Words

Word	Meaning and example
encouragement	
ambition	
stimulation	
influence	
motivation	
innovation	
vision	
unobtrusive	

Main Activity

Start this activity with a definition of the word 'inspiration' – for example, 'the process of being mentally stimulated to do or feel something, especially something creative, helpful and positive.'

Then read the following text, or arrange the children in groups and ask them to read it together. It is about an inspirational inventor – Stephen Davies. He came up with the idea of using new 3D printing technology to produce affordable prosthetic limbs for children.

Stephen Davies's 'Team Unlimbited' Shed is the heart of their charitable business. The shed is where they design, print, build and deliver 3D printed hands and arms for children across the world.

The company was set up after Stephen noticed the huge number of children that had no access, poor choice, or were unable to afford an artificial arm. Team Unlimbited is a completely self-funded business and helps children from all around the world, from Peru to Pakistan, Turkey, Brazil, Chile, Uganda, USA,

Egypt, UK and the USA. All from this unobtrusive little shed, in an unassuming garden, in a small village, nestled in South Wales.

Source: from www.channel4.com

Ask the children to discuss the words below, which will help to build up a schema of the nature of innovation and charitable work:

- bravery
- kindness
- generosity
- vision
- talent.

Next, have a discussion followed by an activity. The children should think of an example of something or somebody who has inspired them. This could be an invention, family member, friend, sporting hero or famous person. After the discussion, they can then produce a piece of text about 100–200 words on that theme. If the children need prompts, suggest athletes they are likely to know, such as Usain Bolt – an iconic sportsman.

After the writing activity, ask the children to read out their passages to the group. Invite comment, discuss and provide feedback.

Optional Activity

Discuss famous inventors and entrepreneurs and research one of these. The passage below should help.

Technological and ideological ideas are essential for progress. Inspirational leaders understand this, and are prone to 'thinking outside the box', as well as encouraging creative and innovative thinking among those they lead. There are many famous ones such as Richard Branson (Virgin companies) and Jackie Stewart (motor racing safety).

Also discuss some additional vocabulary that appears in the passage such as:

- ideological
- prone
- essential.

A further optional activity involves looking at what makes a speech inspirational and identifying this from some examples. Locate an example of an inspirational speech for prompting – for example, Churchill's speeches during the Second World War.

Ask the children to create an inspirational speech, using the following for guidance:

- Have a point (but no more than a few).
- Think about structure (consider ways of planning – e.g. using a mind map).
- Connect and link points.
- Tell a story.
- Rewrite and practise.
- Leave the audience wanting more.

Red Herrings

Red Herring 1

Discuss the meaning of the word 'icon'. It is a word that can be misused – this can also be discussed. An icon could be a pop star or a local community member.

Red Herring 2

Ask the children students to create a mind map using an inspirational character as the main idea. This can be done by putting Post-It notes on to A3 paper. Alternatively, children could use a software program such as Inspiration. The activity can be further developed by using a PowerPoint presentation to discuss inspiring images and subjects.

Tip

Leonardo da Vinci was a monumentally inspirational character with a vision of the future. Exploring the life and times of Leonardo da Vinci can be inspirational.

Websites

Shed of the Year – at www.readersheds.co.uk

George Clarke's Amazing Spaces (TV programme) – at www.channel4.com

Leonardo da Vinci – at www.history.com

Dewey Decimal

300, 670

Apps

People with dyslexia benefit from multi-sensory, active teaching and learning. Technological advances have made it much more possible to adapt lessons to achieve this aim. The range of options is extensive and can be daunting for the busy facilitator. The following app-based activities are based on recommendations from teachers working in a range of contexts.

88 Book Create

The aim of this activity is for the children to produce their own summary of a topic area using BookCreator. With this program, text, images, audio and video can be used to create a range of outputs, including interactive stories, 'about me' books, poetry books, comic books, instruction manuals and science reports. When children create their output, they are engaged in deep processing, and research has shown that this can lead to greater levels of understanding and better recall of a topic area. The output itself can also be used in revision.

Requirements

- access to computer with WiFi and BookCreatorapp (https://bookcreator.com)
- large sheets of paper or computer program, for producing a mind map of the topic

Vocabulary

Verbs: research, construct

Adjectives: imaginary, creative

Nouns: graphics, video

Associated Words

Word	Meaning and example
summarise	
interactive	
multimedia	

Main Activity

The overall task is to produce output that summarises a topic being studied. The content could relate to many areas of the curriculum, including English, history, modern languages, geography, biology and PE.

Children can work independently, or in small groups. First, they will need time to familiarise themselves with the app. Then they produce a mind map of the topic, on paper or using a computer program. They should then decide how best to record the key points.

Optional Activity

Practise mind-mapping. Use the internet for more information about mind maps. The children can then do a mind map theme of their book.

Red Herring

Study a famous author – and try to find out what inspired the author to write a book. Access the internet for ideas.

Dewey Decimal

400

89 Film Create

The aim of this activity is for the children to produce their own summary of a topic area using the iMovie app. Children can make films using an iPhone. They can import these files and then edit and fine-tune them. They can add titles, sound effects and background music.

Requirements

- access to an iPhone and a computer with WiFi, and to the iMovie app (available at www.apple.com)

Vocabulary

Verbs: premiere

Adjective: cutting-room

Nouns: sound effects, graphics

Associated Words

Word	Meaning and example
edit	
fine-tune	
import	

Main Activity

The task is to produce a short video that summarises a topic being studied. The content could relate to many areas of the curriculum, including English, history, modern languages, geography, biology and PE.

Children can work independently or in small groups. First, they need time to familiarise themselves with the app. Then they produce a short film summarising the key points in their chosen area.

Red Herring

Think of your own Red Herring activity! Or ask the children to make one up.

Dewey Decimal

777

90 Green Screen

The aim of this activity is for the children to produce their own video of a topic area, using green screen technology. This allows children to create a background that illustrates the topic they are discussing. This technology is commonly used on TV news and weather reports. When a film is made against a green background, the video can be edited later and a different background can be inserted.

Requirements

- video camera
- green screen (this must be a flat surface – it can be a wall that is painted green or covered in green backing paper, felt or material, or a green screen stand)
- access to a green screen app, such as DoInk (www.doink.com)

Vocabulary

Verbs: edit, superimpose, illustrate

Adjective: professional

Noun: green screen

Associated Words

Word	Meaning and example
imagery	
blending	
producer	

Main Activity

The overall task is to produce short video reporting on a topic being studied. The content could relate to many areas of the curriculum, including English, history, modern languages, geography, biology and PE.

Children should work in small groups. First, they need time to familiarise themselves with the app. Then they should source an appropriate background image or images that will illustrate their report. They produce a short film against the green screen background, and then superimpose different backgrounds – which can include images and videos. With younger children, the facilitator could carry out the editing involved here.

Red Herring

Think of your own Red Herring activity! Or ask the children to make one up.

Dewey Decimal

777

91 iTunes

The aim of this activity is for children to use iTunesU to gather information about a topic. This is helpful for project work and to consolidate work that has already been done for revision. iTunesU features educational audio and video files from universities, museums and public media organisations. It includes resources for primary and secondary school pupils and instructors. This information is also free to download to PCs and mobile devices.

Requirements

- access to computer with WiFi and access to iTunesU (available at https://itunes.apple.com)

Vocabulary

Verb: research

Adjective: relevant

Noun: resource

Associated Words

Word	Meaning and example
develop	
public media	
download	

Main Activity

The task is to pick a topic area and to use iTunesU to find content that is relevant to the child's area of interest.

Children can work independently or in small groups. First, they will need time to familiarise themselves with iTunesU. Then they should produce a list of relevant items, noting the web links and summarising the content.

Red Herring

Think of your own Red Herring activity! Or ask the children to make one up.

Dewey Decimal

370

92 Review the Apps

The aim of this activity is to review apps that are available to help children with dyslexic difficulties. This activity can be repeated with the same group, if different categories of app are chosen.

Requirements

- access to computers to open and try different apps
- CALL Scotland Wheel of iPad Apps for Learners with Dyslexia/Reading and Writing Difficulties (available at www.callscotland.org.uk). There is also a CALL Scotland Wheel of Android Apps for Learners with Dyslexia/Reading and Writing Difficulties (also available at www.callscotland.org.uk).

- paper/digital recorders for taking notes
- review sheets (details provided below)

Vocabulary

Verbs: review, compare, rate

Adjectives: helpful, effective

Nouns: assistive technology, qualities

Associated Words

Word	Meaning and example
critical	
universal	
rating	

Main Activity

The task is to work in teams to compare different assistive technology apps that are designed to help learners with dyslexia/reading and writing difficulties.

Distribute copies of the CALL Scotland 'Wheel of Apps' for learners with dyscalculia/numeracy difficulties, available at: www.callscotland.org.uk

Distribute review sheets. Allow space for the children to note their responses to the following questions:

- What is the app designed to do?
- What is the target audience?
- What does the app do? What does it not do?

Use the following star rating:

***** = highly recommended

**** = very useful

*** = useful

** = not useful

* = not recommended.

Apps should be given separate scores under the following suggested headings (these can be added to or amended):

- easy to understand
- easy to use
- helpful.

Start by going through the categories that are noted on the Wheel of Apps:

- early reading
- talking books
- creating stories
- text to speech
- reading ebooks
- working with PDFs
- scanning
- letter formation/handwriting
- sentence structure
- word predictors
- note-taking
- audio notes
- word processing
- speech recognition
- calculator
- mathematics
- mind-mapping
- outlining
- information gathering
- improving memory
- reminders.

After discussion with the children, choose which categories might be most useful to them at their stage.

In groups, children should start by making notes about what they might like to see in an app. For example, what elements of a maths task do they find hard?

Children should then try out the apps one by one, taking notes and discussing them in their groups. Each group could work on a different set of apps, or groups could review the same apps. Once this is done, they could present their findings to the rest of their peers.

Red Herring

Think of your own Red Herring activity! Or ask the children to make one up.

Dewey Decimal

600

93 Birds

This activity is geared to motivation and creativity, as well as developing children's knowledge of birds. It is a practical activity and involves the child using imagination and improvisation skills. The focus is on a multi-sensory activity that involves making a model bird.

This activity will take a few sessions to complete.

Requirements

- coathanger wire
- pliers
- newspaper
- clay
- cardboard/card
- masking tape
- water
- paint brushes
- superglue
- Modroc (optional – if using Modroc, follow health and safety guidance and use adequate surface protection for table tops)
- scraps of fabric (optional)
- small block of wood (optional – to produce a stand for the bird)

Vocabulary

Verb: bend

Adjective: frightening

Noun: bird

Associated Words

Word	Meaning and example
model	
manipulate	
malleable	
craft	
form	
aerodynamics	
glide	

Main Activity

Ask the children to access images of birds, either in hard copy from the library or on the internet. They should photocopy or print out an image to work from when constructing their model bird. Alternatively, provide a selection of images for the children to choose from, or some children might like to work from their own drawings.

Depending on resources available, the birds can be formed from wire bent into shape and then built up using paper, card or scrap fabric and tape. Children can be as creative and imaginative as they like. The model could be a hybrid bird.

There is the option to mount the birds on a block of wood, or attach to a piece of branch from a tree. If mounting on a block of wood, it is useful to be able to drill a hole or holes in the wood, so that wire from the bird's feet can be put through to secure the model. Alternatively, the model can be glued to the block.

Scrap material can be used to decorate the birds, and there is scope for imagination here.

Optional Activity

Watch Alfred Hitchcock's film *The Birds* (1963). The genre is horror, and this horror film is set in America. It focuses on a series of sudden, unexplained, violent attacks on people by birds and swarms of birds. This film is great for prompting discussion and interest.

Red Herring

Make a paper aeroplane and discuss its properties and what makes a successful model, looking at style, aerodynamics and distance achieved.

Tip

Utilise Modroc and any other useful resources. Libraries can be useful for old newspapers. If using clay for detail, completely cover it with Modroc while the clay is still moist.

Bird models can be used to teach size, field marks, anatomy, pattern and colour.

Websites

Wire modelling ideas – at www.pinterest.com

Bird project ideas – at www.pinterest.com

Film review of *The Birds* – at www.filmsite.org

The Birds (film) – at https://en.wikipedia.org

Amusing birds – at www.youtube.com

Dewey Decimal

598, 730

94 Summaries

The aim of this activity is for the children to produce their own summary of a topic. They can use the iMovie app, or some other similar app they are familiar with.

They should try to make it concise and attention-grabbing. It is important to remind them that it is a summary – like the trailer for a movie. They can watch some trailers of current films – these are readily available on cinema websites.

Requirements

- access to an iPhone and a computer with WiFi, and access to the iMovie app (available at www.apple.com)

Vocabulary

Verbs: edit, fine-tune

Adjective: oscar-winning

Noun: sound effects

Associated Words

Word	Meaning and example
trailer	
concise	
dramatic	

Main Activity

The task is to produce a short video that summarises a topic being studied. The content could relate to many areas of the curriculum, including English, history, modern languages, geography, biology and PE.

Children can work independently or in small groups. First, they need time to familiarise themselves with the app. Then they produce a short film summarising the key points in their chosen area.

Optional Activity

Arrange a film afternoon or evening – complete with popcorn and drinks!

Red Herring

The children should identify a movie that is available on the internet – often they have extras that give information on how the movie was shot and interviews with the cast. They can then watch this and summarise some of the challenges in making a movie.

Websites

How to make a movie – at www.wikihow.com

Learn about film: making a movie – at http://learnaboutfilm.com

Dewey Decimal

777

95 Metal

Learning is all about experiences, and particularly varied experiences. Experiencing different and new situations can help to harness creativity and extend learning. The aim of this activity is to provide experiences in working with metal, discussing different metal types and understanding the importance of metal and how it has been produced and used through the different ages.

Requirements

- hammer
- centre punch
- hacksaw
- metal files
- G-clamp or vice
- hand drill
- scrap metal pieces for working – aluminium is recommended
- safety goggles

Vocabulary

Verb: drill

Adjective: precious

Noun: hacksaw

Associated Words

Word	Meaning and example
gold	
bronze	
iron	
Iron Age	
tin	
ferrous	
non-ferrous	
aluminium	
magnet	
ore	
copper	

Main Activity

Clamp a piece of metal in a vice or G-clamp and use a hacksaw (metal saw) to saw the piece of metal in half. Using a file, smooth the ends of the piece of metal as evenly as possible.

After putting on safety goggles, the children can try to drill a piece of soft metal such as aluminium. The piece of aluminium will need to have a target point on it. This is done by striking the centre punch with the hammer on to the clamped aluminium piece. This mark/indent will now act as a guide for the drill bit, and it means the drill will go through the metal at that point and will not slip.

Bronze Age Britain

It is believed that the Bronze Age in Britain occurred around 2000 BC.

It is thought that Britain was influenced by the peoples of Europe, and this was a catalyst for the Bronze Age. Previously, Britons used stone for tools. True bronze is a combination of 10% tin and 90% copper, and both materials were readily available in Britain around this time. Find out more about this from the internet.

Ask the children to investigate the following topics and share their findings:

- production: how metal is mined/produced
- timeline: metal through history
- agriculture: metal and farming
- transport: cars, boats, planes, trains
- arts: sculpture, casting and welding
- weapons: armour.

Optional Activity

The Use of Steel

The use of steel is a more recent development. Steel frames were used for dwellings in the late 19th century and, of course, throughout the 20th century.

Children should look at the history of steel buildings on the following website, investigate the topics and share their findings: http://jameswareconstructioninc.com

As a quiz option, ask the children to focus on three facts to memorise and then be tested on.

Children can make up some quizzes of their own.

Red Herring

The Olympic Games are famous for its medals – gold, silver and bronze. Winning Olympic gold has become the highest accolade a sportsperson can achieve.

Use the internet to try to work out how these medals originated.

Tip

Access the short YouTube clip called 'Welcome to Metal Tip and Tricks' and discuss the various aspects of it.

Websites

Gold facts – at www.scienceforkidsclub.com

Ten fun facts about gold – at www.sbcgold.com

History of steel buildings – at http://jameswareconstructioninc.com

Dewey Decimal

600, 730

96 Telephone/Mobile

This form of communication has revolutionised the way we interact and access information. At the same time, it can also be seen as a resource for supporting learning. Through this activity, children can develop an appreciation of this technological invention and how they can use it to strengthen their learning styles and skills. The smartphone can be used as a means of recording, note-taking and visual capture for recall and revision/study skills.

Requirements

- mobile phones
- local visitor attraction leaflets

Vocabulary

Verb: text

Adjective: articulate

Noun: mobile phone

Associated Words

Word	Meaning and example
telephone	
texting	

mobile	
messaging	
elocution	
receiver	

Main Activity

As a life-skill exercise, the children can be asked to use a mobile phone to find out information about a local attraction. It can be daunting to speak over the phone to someone you don't know, and by doing this confidence can be enhanced. This practice can also be integrated into a group visit to the attraction. Questions that are relevant to the nature of the attraction and the group's requirements can be prepared in advance. This can be discussed ahead of the trip.

Download a passage about Alexander Graham Bell or ask the children to access online. They will note that Alexander Graham Bell was a Scottish-born American scientist and inventor and was most famous for the development of the telephone. Bell also invented the metal detector.

Once they have read this, they should, in small groups, work out a timeline of Bell's life and highlight the key points in the development of the telephone.

Optional Activity

The Mobile Phone

Children should access the internet or print out key passages and develop a time line from the early telephone to modern mobile phones.

Red Herring

The first intelligible words ever transmitted by telephone were 'Mr Watson – come here – I want to see you.'

These words were spoken by Alexander Graham Bell, inventor of the telephone, when he made the first call on 10 March 1876, to his assistant, Thomas Watson.

Ask the children: 'What would you have said?'

The Royal High School

Alexander Graham Bell attended the Royal High School in Edinburgh. The building still stands today but not as a school – as government offices. The school has moved to more modern premises.

The Royal High has a long and interesting history – find out about this on the internet, and note any key facts about the history of the Royal High.

Tip

The mobile phone can be a tremendous resource for all children to support their learning styles and capture data for strengthening their knowledge base. As technology develops, the mobile phone will be an increasingly indispensable resource, used in tandem with other learning methods.

Website

Using mobile phones in classroom teaching – at www.theguardian.com

Dewey Decimal

600

Home and School

Introduction

Home and school are inextricably linked, and this can be extremely beneficial for the child with dyslexia. Where activities are carried out at school, they can be carried over to home. This can represent overlearning, which has already been noted in this book as a key factor for children with dyslexia.

We have endeavoured to ensure that many of the activities in this book can be carried out at home. Although some of them focus on group work, they can just as easily be carried out at home on an individual basis. This section just highlights some specific activities for home, and the activities are just as relevant for parents as for other facilitators.

97 Shades of Colours

This activity can be tailored for a range of ages, but the example below is geared towards younger children. For older children, the activity can become one of colour appreciation and manipulation rather than colour recognition.

The aim of this activity is to help young children to acquire automaticity in recognising colours, and how colours can mix to form other colours. The activity in this form can help with colour naming and with visual appreciation. For older children, it can become an activity in art appreciation, and an analysis of the colours used by painters and what the colours depict – for example, mood. The aim of this aspect of the activity would be to gain some insight into the painter, and perhaps the reason why they painted this particular picture. For older children, this can help with analytical thinking and looking beyond the picture. This is similar to inferential reading, when the reader looks beyond the print.

Requirements

- colour charts – these can be used by painting squares of colour on to a large sheet of paper, or paint charts can be collected from DIY stores and photocopied to increase the size; if using paint charts, you will need two sets of each – one for cutting out, and one for reference
- art paper
- selection of paints
- paint brushes
- images of paintings (for older children)

Vocabulary

The vocabulary can be tailored for different age ranges but examples are shown below:

Verb: draw

Adjective: colourful

Noun: artist

Associated Words

Word	Meaning and example
paintbrush	
easel	
stroke	
mix	
soft	
frame	

Main Activity

Provide the children with colour charts (keeping one set of each type of chart for reference), then ask them to do the following. It can be useful to work in pairs.

1. Cut out all the different colours and shades.

2. Place all the similar colours together.

3. Select one colour, arrange the shades from light to dark, and glue these in order on to a piece of art paper.

4. Write the names of the colours (given on the colour shade card; they may need to check back to the reference charts).

5. Choose one shade from the card and mix colours from the paint provided to copy the correct shade.

Optional Activity

The whole group could do a montage of colours and shades for display on the wall.

Red Herring (for older children)

Children should collect pictures from the internet of 'old masters' or modern paintings. They can then refer to a colour card and try to name the colour or approximation of the colours used, and then comment on why the painter used those colours. What image do the colours convey?

Dewey Decimal

740

98 North, South, East, West

Two aspects that can cause difficulty for children with dyslexia are directional confusion and naming speed. For example, they can often confuse left and right, or up and down. Similarly, they can have difficulties with compass points – north, south, east and west. Practising these can be good for generalising the skill to other areas relating to directions, etc. There is also research that indicates that dyslexic children may take longer to access the label or name of an item. Practice at processing speed can therefore be useful for all children with dyslexia.

The aim of this activity is to help children to develop automaticity in recognising directions, and to practise responding to questions at speed. It can therefore help with reaction speed.

Requirements

- compass
- removable, blank stickers
- instruction sheets (described below)
- pencils – several sets of 20 different colours, or, if fewer colours are available, pencils and small, coloured stickers (see below)
- timer

Vocabulary

Verb: direct

Adjective: speedy

Noun: map

Associated Words

Word	Meaning and example
compass	
North Pole	
Pole Star	
astronomy	
astrology	
mariner	

Main Activity

Directional Orientation

This is done in the form of a game, with children in groups of three. Using a compass, they should signpost the following directional points: north, north-east, north-west, south, south-east and south-west. They should put their own removable stickers at these points so they can recognise them.

Each group is given different colour pencils – if you don't have enough colours, place different colours of tape over each pencil. This means you can have the red pencil with blue tape or the red pencil with green tape, etc.

It is important that each group has the same combination of pencils and colour-coded (taped) pencils. Try to get at least 20 for each group – if you do not have enough pencils, using other objects is fine as long as each group has identical objects.

Work with one group at a time. Give the first group the instruction sheet indicating which pencil to put in which part of the room – for example, red pencil with green tape in the north-west. Using a timer, make a note of the time that each group takes to complete the task. Repeat this with the remaining groups.

It is important that the instruction sheet is made up in advance. It is a good idea to pilot it yourself, to get an idea of a benchmark time.

Optional Activity

You can make this more difficult by adding, for example, south-south-west, or easier by using just the four points of the compass.

Red Herring

Think of your own Red Herring activity! Or ask the children to make one up.

Dewey Decimal

910

99 Which Way?

Children with dyslexia can have a word-finding difficulty, and may not be able to articulate exactly what they mean because they cannot find the exact word. Exercises to help with word-finding and accurately describing an object or event are extremely useful. One such example that can be used with children is giving and receiving directions. This is the focus of this activity.

The aim of this activity is to help children with dyslexia to become more familiar with the vocabulary used in giving concise and accurate directions, and to use it in a meaningful context. As an additional factor, this activity can also help with grammar and prepositions.

Requirements

- a set of tourist maps for each group
- glossaries for landmarks and prepositions (some are provided below, for guidance)

Vocabulary

Verb: adjoin

Adjective: long

Noun: crossroads

Associated Words

Word	Meaning and example
compass	
junction	
precinct	
pedestrian	
cul-de-sac	
orientation	

Main Activity

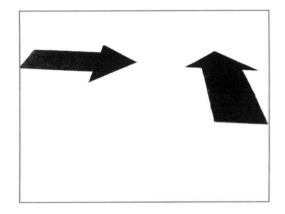 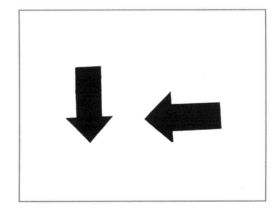

This is done in the form of a game, with the children in pairs.

Provide the children with a series of glossaries – an example is shown below:

Glossary – Some Landmarks

taxi rank = a place where taxis queue for passengers

level crossing = where the road and railway meet. There are barriers that go up and down to signal when a train is coming

underpass = a walkway that goes under a busy road so pedestrians can get to the other side safely

overpass/flyover = a road that goes over another road (or railway)

zebra crossing = black-and-white markings in the road for pedestrians to cross the road (the markings look like a zebra's stripes)

pedestrian crossing = a place in the road where pedestrians can cross; often there are traffic lights

tunnel = a road under (or through) mountains

crossroads = where two roads cross each other

junction = where one road meets another, and you can either go left or right

fork in the road = where the road divides, and you decide to go left or right

turning = a road off to your left or right

main road = a big road where there is lots of traffic

lane = a small road, or a part of a road (the left-hand lane, the right-hand lane, the bus lane)

Make up a glossary of prepositions – for example, 'along', 'down', 'through' and 'opposite'.

1. Ask the children to form pairs.

2. Give each pair a tourist map of their town or nearest city. Some key places of interest should be noted.

3. Divide the group into two (with children still working in pairs). Each pair will take turns at being 'tourists'.

4. Each pair of tourists decides where it is they want to go.

5. Each pair of tourists then assigns themselves to a pair from the other group and asks for directions.

6. The tourists then have to grade the direction-givers. They can allocate a maximum of two points for each of the following criteria (maximum total = eight points):

    - manners and approachability

    - clarity of language

    - accuracy of directions

    - confidence in their response.

7. Groups should swap roles and repeat so that each pair has the chance to give directions.

Optional Activity

All groups with maximum points or the three groups with the highest number of points should then act out their performance to the rest of their peers. The children then give them marks, using the same criteria.

Red Herring

Think of your own Red Herring activity! Or ask the children to make one up.

Tip

This activity may get a bit noisy, so it is a good idea to try to find some other locations nearby where some groups can go.

Dewey Decimal

910

100 Metro Paper

The message we always give to children and to parents who often ask what they can do to help their child's reading is: read regularly – every day – even if it is a small piece of text, or newspaper item. We emphasise the newspaper part because newspapers are readily available, and they offer a choice of articles from current affairs to sports. Usually, the reader will find something of interest in the newspaper. For this activity, we have selected the *Metro* because it is a free newspaper in the UK – other countries will have similar free newspapers.

The aim of this activity is to develop in children the habit of reading for pleasure and purpose. Additionally, it provides the opportunity for the children to enhance their understanding about current and contemporary issues. This activity can also be followed up by using different newspapers.

Requirements

- daily newspapers, bought or free (the *Metro* is a good example of a free newspaper)

Vocabulary

Verb: read

Adjective: concise

Noun: newspaper

Associated Words

Word	Meaning and example
media	
caption	
image	
layout	
headline	
article	
tabloid	

Main Activity

This activity will include reading for pleasure, shared reading and reading aloud. This activity can be used to support curricular studies and English language skills.

Procedure

1. Buy in newspapers, or collect free media papers – try to get at least one copy of the same newspaper for each child.

2. Distribute the newspapers to the group, and ask each child to select one article from the paper.

3. In turn, each child comments on their choice, informing the others of the name of the article and the page to find it on.

4. All children then find the article in question to read – the children can read aloud if they are OK with this, or reading can be silent.

5. Comment on the use of headlines, pictures, colour, captions and specific vocabulary.

6. Ask the children to make headings for each of the above.

Optional Activity

Write a fictional article for a tabloid, with headline, image, caption and credit. This could be typed, and computer programs can be used for creative layouts.

Red Herring

Sports sections are generally found at the back of newspapers, and they provide the opportunity to discuss a variety of sports, including those that children might participate in. They may even be members of different sports clubs. This could lead on to a discussion of other clubs they are part of, such as drama, music or photography. The sharing of these activities provides an excellent platform for talking, listening and sharing. The discussion can extend to holidays and some interesting sports/activities children have participated in.

Tip

Free local papers can be found on buses, in railway stations and airports, and in various information outlets.

The website www.theday.com is a good resource for global up-to-date daily news and extended exercises supporting comprehension. This is a subscription site, and is recommended for whole-group access.

Websites

News from the BBC – www.bbc.co.uk

The Metro (newspaper) – www.metro.co.uk

The Day (news website) – www.theday.com

Dewey Decimal

070

101   Just Breathe

Children with dyslexia can experience anxiety in many different types of situations. It is a good idea to be aware of this, because it is rarely obvious.

The aim of the activity is to encourage children to be aware of the role and importance of relaxation, and how to monitor and take some control over their own body, particularly in relation to breathing. This activity can be ideal at the start of the day or at the end of the day to help them unwind!

Requirements

- There are no specific requirements for this activity but it is a good idea to ensure the children have a calm space with minimal or no background noise.

Vocabulary

Verb: breathe

Adjective: relaxing

Noun: triangle

Associated Words

Word	Meaning and example
relaxation	
self-monitoring	
anxious	
frustration	
tension	
self-awareness	

Main Activity

1. Ask the children to sit in an upright position.

2. Illustrate the shape of a triangle (pizza slice) by modelling this in the air. Alternatively, draw a pizza slice on cardboard and cut it out.

3. Ask the children, using an index finger, to practise drawing the triangle (pizza slice) in the air. They should do this about four times to achieve some familiarity with the sequence.

4. Model the following sequence of breathing, while air-drawing the pizza shape:

    - down – **breathe in** and count to four

    - up – **hold breath** for four

    - then top of pizza crust – **breathe** out for four.

5. Repeat the cycle four or five times. During this practice, you should be saying the instructions softly. This is important because children can lose track of the cycle.

Eventually, the children will be able to do this without being monitored.

Children can design and cut out their own pizza slice. They can then use this to help with their own breathing, particularly when they feel anxious.

Optional Activity

Children can also look at other ways of controlling breathing. Also, progressive relaxation can be taught. There are a number of excellent videos to choose from on the internet.

Red Herring

Ask the children to find out about pizzas. Where did they originate? Why are the slices triangular? List some of the ingredients of pizza.

The internet can be used as a prompt, or you can print out an article for the children.

Websites

History of pizza – at www.lifeinitaly.com

Breathing exercises for children – at https://move-with-me.com

How to teach your child calm breathing (for parents) – at www.anxietybc.com

Dewey Decimal

100, 613.79

Dewey Decimal Numbers

1. **Music and Lyrics**
   781

2. **Nato Phonetic Alphabet**
   470, 471

3. **Letters, Words and Sentences**
   403

4. **All about the Horse**
   636

5. **Reading for Purpose**
   610

6. **Genre**
   200, 910

7. **Information Leaflet**
   900

8. **Spelling Corks**
   400, 794, 795

9. **Spelling Golf**
   400, 794, 795

10. **Spelling Ping-Pong**
    400, 794, 795

11. **Spelling – Be a Teacher**
    403

12. **Target Words and Visual Connections**
    400, 753

13. **Syllables, Syllables, Syllables**
    421

14. **Churchill**
    940.53

15. **Frame It**
    807

16. **Snippets and More**
    807

17. **Be a Script Writer**
    777

18. **Creative Writing Pockets**
    372.6

19. **Rubber Band – A Writing Prompt**
    730

20. **Bananas**
    634

21. **Tunnock's Teacake**
    641.86

22. **VCOP (Vocabulary, Connectives, Openers, Punctuation)**
    400

23. **Local Language**
    400

24. **Forest Walk**
    400, 508, 577

25. **'A' is for...**
    400

26. **Poetry Path**
    530.8

27. **Word Wheel**
400, 403

28. **Nouns – Flashcards**
426, 428

29. **Taste Texts**
394.1

30. **Keys**
600, 620

31. **Tongue Twisters**
790

32. **Pirates**
364.1

33. **UFOs (Unidentified Flying Objects)**
001.942

34. **Yellow**
150, 750

35. **Black**
150, 520, 750

36. **Dodo**
560, 580, 590

37. **Trees**
580, 710

38. **Water**
500, 551.3, 610

39. **Circus**
790

40. **Sweets**
610, 760

41. **Stunts**
790

42. **What's New/Interesting/ Forgettable?**
070

43. **Time**
600

44. **Volcanoes**
551.2

45. **Critical Thinking**
150

46. **Celebrity 'Mastermind'**
030

47. **Pictures Say 100 Words**
740, 750

48. **Share for Success – 'Helping Me, Helping You'**
302, 303

49. **We've Got Talent**
790, 791, 792

50. **Self-Portrait**
743

51. **Quizzes**
030

52. **Superstitions**
130

53. **List the Lists**
150, 153

54. **Kim's Game**
150, 153

55. **Picture Card Prompts**
750, 770

56. **Pelmanism**
790

57. **The Kluge**
530, 600, 790

58. **Smells**
150, 570

59. **Ellipse**
513.21

60. **Framing**
340, 600

61. Visual Spatial
710, 780, 790

62. Armchair Olympics
796

63. City Trip
910

64. Overseas Trip
910

65. Design a Den
729

66. Adjective Wall
400

67. PT (Position and Time) Prepositions
400

68. Use My Name
403

69. Verbs Charade
403

70. Who Am I?
408

71. Culture and Customs
390, 391

72. Idioms
400

73. Opposites
400

74. Diamante Poetry
400

75. What We Eat
641

76. Dewey Decimal System
001

77. Spinneracy
400

78. Using the Whole Brain
100–199

79. Badge-Making
690

80. Questioning Questions
352.3

81. Sounds
781

82. FreeRice
381.4, 633.18

83. Annotation
370

84. Knots
514

85. Film
600, 700

86. Animation
777

87. Inspiration
300, 670

88. Book Create
400

89. Film Create
777

90. Green Screen
777

91. iTunes
370

92. Review the Apps
600

93. Birds
598, 730

94. Summaries
777

95. Metal
600, 730

96. Telephone/Mobile
600

97. Shades of Colours
740

98. North, South, East, West
910

99. Which Way?
910

100. *Metro* Paper
070

101. Just Breathe
100, 613.79

Vocabulary Used in Activities

1. Music and Lyrics
orchestra
stanza
couplet
lyrics
composer
arrangement

2. Nato Phonetic Alphabet
sequence
memorable
vocalise
association
North Atlantic Treaty
  Organization (NATO)

3. Letters, Words and Sentences
listen
sound
rhyme
sense

4. All about the Horse
reins
saddle
transport
racing
stirrup
stable
annotation

5. Reading for Purpose
syrup
lion
GDA (Guideline Daily Amount)
sweetness
strength
connotation

6. Genre
category
class
group
bracket
variety
type
style

7. Information Leaflet
poster
attraction
indulge
pamphlet

8. Spelling Corks
practice
balance
land
turn
repeat
complete

9. Spelling Golf
aim
putter
grip
speed
accuracy
points
shot

10. Spelling Ping-Pong
net
ball
bat
score
table
tennis
hit
gently
sequence

11. Spelling – Be a Teacher
weather
forecast
litter
climate
tornado

12. Target Words and Visual Connections
green
tree
grass
peas

13. Syllables, Syllables, Syllables
syllable
clap
method
realise
count

14. Churchill
steadfast
leader
inspiration
defiant
popular
stature
politician

15. Frame It
analyse
discuss
compare
dissect
conclude
compelling

16. Snippets and More
crowd
tone
angry
unusual
serious

17. Be a Script Writer
In this activity, the children provide the associated words.

18. Creative Writing Pockets
mask
ticket
key

rag
map
wrapper
bulb

19. Rubber Band – A Writing Prompt
snap
expand
ping
restrict
hold

20. Bananas
ripe
fibre
juicy
enjoy
sweet

21. Tunnock's Teacake
delicious
chocolate
bite
sweet
aftertaste
impression
anticipate

22. VCOP (Vocabulary, Connectives, Openers, Punctuation)
vocabulary
connective
opener
punctuation
structure
visualise

23. Local Language
display
quotation
locality
feelings
intangible

24. Forest Walk
snail
squirrel
rustle
deep
branch
perimeter

25. 'A' is for...
display
folder
text
presentation
quantity
accuracy

26. Poetry Path
traffic
sound
aroma
bird
tree
colour
locality

27. Word Wheel
wheel
puzzle
diagram
image

28. Nouns – Flashcards
guess
describe
adjective
alight

29. Taste Texts
scratch
seasonal
shortcut
tasting
subliminal

30. Keys
lock
unique
musical
management
topic
torque
recruited

31. Tongue Twisters
articulation
sequence
pronunciation
alliteration
concentration
amusement

32. Pirates
treasure
gold
swashbuckling
buccaneer
plank
eye patch
piracy
combating

33. UFOs (Unidentified Flying Objects)
space
atmosphere
universe
terrestrial
planet
alien
imagination

34. Yellow
ochre
tone
shade
emotion
season
connotation
optimism
clarity

35. Black
black
noir
Dark Ages
pitch black
black arts
charcoal
coal
shade
black out
blacksmith
black-and-white photography

36. Dodo
extinct
icon
appearance
account
caricature
responsible

37. Trees
bark
branch
bud
leaf
trunk
wood
forest
crop
paper
pulp
carve

38. Water
steam
sea
distilled
boiling point
rain
spring
health
dehydrate
refract
ice

39. Circus
big top
clown
acrobat
ring master
trapeze artist
daredevil
lion tamer
animal cruelty
illusionist
contortionist
parade
publicity
balance

40. Sweets
sucrose
fructose
sugar
slavery
health
diabetes
marketing
confectionery
chewy
boiled
sweet tooth
fruit

41. Stunts
spectacular
stunt
daring
dangerous
publicity
elaborate
parachute
skilled
audacious

42. What's New/Interesting/ Forgettable?
edition
press
compose
classified
feature
media

43. Time
duration
measurement
precise
compare
sequence
past
countdown
watch
present

44. Volcanoes
Vesuvius
force
lava
Pompeii
eruption
gas
catastrophe

45. Critical Thinking
critical
observation
interpretation
creative
reflection
organisation
evaluation
inference
question
mental
decision
construct

46. Celebrity 'Mastermind'
specialist
pass
participation
championship
depth
bank of questions

47. Pictures Say 100 Words
detail
paint
outline
mass
merge
background

**48. Share for Success –
'Helping Me, Helping You'**
discussion
communicate
support
teamwork

49. We've Got Talent
competition
judge
participation
audience
voting
compere

50. Self-Portrait
observe
draw
focus
ellipse
symmetrical
balance

51. Quizzes
clue
questioning
create
equivalent
request
appropriate
relevant
nonsense

52. Superstitions
omen
belief
credible
supernatural
irrational
ominous

53. List the Lists
recap
checklist
elaborate
priority
category

54. Kim's Game
noun
memory
speed
recall
association
remember
grouping

55. Picture Card Prompts
image
content
colour
scene
story
annotate
graphic novel

56. Pelmanism
concentration
matching
attention
memory
shuffling
anagram

57. The Kluge
skill
daring
memorable
precarious
incredible
ingenuity
implausible
contrivance

58. Smells
scent
fragrance
aroma
pungent
acute
lingering
glomerulus
odour

59. Ellipse
ellipse stage
circle
plane
curve

60. Framing
mitre
saw (noun)
glue
join
measure
clamp
bond
precise
bleed

61. Visual Spatial
organisation
assembly
reasoning
planning
calculating
surveying

62. Armchair Olympics
Olympic
Paralympic
athlete
achievement
honour
perseverance
sensational
cumulative

63. City Trip
prioritise
feasible
schedule
tourist attraction
marketing

64. Overseas Trip
budget
time zone
currency
airport
passport
visa

65. Design a Den
area
scale
angle
dimension
space-saving

66. Adjective Wall
scan
select
variety
novel
decorative
elaborate

67. PT (Position and Time) Prepositions
sentence stem
position
bingo
appropriate
between
beneath

68. Use My Name
define
describe
discuss
gregarious
intelligent
thoughtful

69. Verbs Charade
mime
pretend
guess
hilarious
clue

70. Who Am I?
occupation
action
gesture
posture

71. Culture and Customs
annual
religious
culture
custom
traditional
relation
historical
artefact
stereotype

72. Idioms
spilt
mustard
lining
grapevine
grain

73. Opposites
opposite
differ
contrast
extreme
similar

74. Diamante Poetry
diamante
synonym
diamond
brainstorm
descriptive

75. What We Eat
harvest
import
export
tariff
ripe
famine

76. Dewey Decimal System
classification
searching
sequence
demonstration

77. Spinneracy
hyperbole
onomatopoeia
connective
pun

78. Using the Whole Brain
whole brain
ambidextrous
hemisphere
simultaneous
visual

79. Badge-Making
create
draw
pressure
design
align

80. Questioning Questions
interrogate
enquire
inquest
rhetorical

81. Sounds
melodic
rhythmical
bang
haunting
clunk/clink
buzz

82. FreeRice
rice
charity
famine
support
giving

83. Annotation
notes
explanation
recurrent
specific
points

84. Knots
reef knot
granny knot
clove hitch
butterfly knot
figure-eight knot
cow hitch
fisherman knot

85. Film
actor
prop
lighting
costume
drama
scene
script
director
designer

86. Animation
cartoon
project (verb)
character
storyboard
viewing
technique

87. Inspiration
encouragement
ambition
stimulation
influence
motivation
innovation
vision
unobtrusive

88. Book Create
summarise
interactive
multimedia

89. Film Create
edit
fine-tune
import

90. Green Screen
imagery
blending
producer

91. iTunes
develop
public media
download

92. Review the Apps
critical
universal
rating

93. Birds
model
manipulate
malleable
craft
form
aerodynamics
glide

94. Summaries
trailer
concise
dramatic

95. Metal
gold
bronze
iron
Iron Age
tin
ferrous
non-ferrous
aluminium
magnet
ore
copper

96. Telephone/Mobile
telephone
texting
mobile
messaging
elocution
receiver

97. Shades of Colours
paintbrush
easel
stroke
mix
soft
frame

98. North, South, East, West
compass
North Pole
Pole Star
astronomy
astrology
mariner

99. Which Way?
compass
junction
precinct
pedestrian
cul-de-sac
orientation

100. _Metro_ Paper
media
caption
image

layout
headline
article
tabloid

101. Just Breathe
relaxation
self-monitoring
anxious
frustration
tension
self-awareness

References

Peer, L. and Reid, G. (2016) *Multilingualism, Literacy and Dyslexia: Breaking Down Barriers for Educators*, 2nd edition. Routledge.

Reid, G. (2016) *Dyslexia: A Practitioner's Handbook*, 5th edition. Chichester: John Wiley & Sons.

West, T. G. (2017) *Seeing What Others Cannot See: The Hidden Advantages of Visual Thinkers and Differently Wired Brains.* New York: Prometheus Books.

Index

'A' is for... 84–5
activities 12–14
   framework 15–16
   red herrings 14–15
adjectives 13, 94
   Adjective Wall 212–14
   Diamante Poetry 231–3
   Use My Name 217–19
advertisements 35
All about the Horse 27–9
alliteration 25, 77, 98, 242
Animation 264–6
Annotation 256–8
anxiety 10
   Just Breathe 300–1
Armchair Olympics 200–2
articulation 97
automaticity 9–10, 25, 102, 219, 229
   'A' is for... 84–5
   Keys 94–7
   North, South, East, West 292–4
   PT (Position and Time) Prepositions 214–17
   Word Wheel 88–90

Badge-Making 245–7
Bananas 71–3
Be a Script Writer 64–6
Birds 278–80
Black 115–18
books 32
   Book Create 270–1
brain use 243
   Using the Whole Brain 243–5

Celebrity 'Mastermind' 152–4
Churchill 56–9
Circus 128–30
City Trip 203–5
colour 111
   Black 115–18
   Shades of Colours 290–2
   Yellow 111–15
comprehension 12, 14, 17, 80, 102, 140
   Celebrity 'Mastermind' 152–4
   Critical Thinking 148–50
   Forest Walk 80–2
   Pirates 106–9

   Spinneracy 241–3
   Time 142–5
   Volcanoes 145–8
   What's New/Interesting/Forgettable? 140–1
concentration 97, 251
   Tongue Twisters 97–9
confidence 10, 44
   Questioning Questions 247–50
   Spelling Ping-Pong 44–6
   Tongue Twisters 97–9
   VCOP (Vocabulary, Connectives, Openers, Punctuation 76–8
coordination 10
   Circus 128–30
   Spelling Corks 40–2
   Spelling Golf 42–4
creative writing 18, 47, 186, 253, 265
   Creative Writing Pockets 66–8
   VCOP (Vocabulary, Connectives, openers, Punctuation 76–8
creativity 10, 11, 12, 14, 18, 60
   Animation 264–6
   Birds 278–80
   Book Create 270–1
   Film Create 271–2
   Green Screen 273–4
   Inspiration 266–70
   iTunes 274–5
   Metal 282–5
   Review the Apps 275–8
   Summaries 280–2
   Telephone/Mobile 285–7
Critical Thinking 148–50
Culture and Customs 223–6

Design a Den 208–10
Dewey Decimal system 15
   Dewey Decimal System activity 238–40
Diamante Poetry 231–3
directional skills 292, 294
   North, South, East, West 292–4
   Which Way? 294–7
Dodo 118–21
dyslexia 9
   barriers to learning 10–11
   difficulties across the curriculum 11, 189–90
   what works best 9–10

Ellipse 192–4
emotive language 92
English as a Second Language (ESL) 211
English as an Additional Language (EAL) 211
    Adjective Wall 212–14
    Culture and Customs 223–6
    Diamante Poetry 231–3
    Idioms 226–9
    Opposites 229–31
    PT (Position and Time) Prepositions 214–17
    Use My Name 217–19
    Verbs Charade 219–21
    Who Am I? 221–3
executive functioning difficulties 10
expressive writing 10, 56, 71, 78, 56, 71, 78
    see also written expression

Film 260–2
Film Create 271–2
Forest Walk 80–2
Frame It 60–2
Framing 194–6
FreeRice 253–5

games 12, 26, 40, 44, 84, 102, 103
    Kim's Game 174–6
    Pelmanism 178–80
    Pictures Say 100 Words 156–7
    Quizzes 164–6
    Self-Portrait 162–4
    Share for Success – 'Helping Me, Helping You' 157–9
    Spelling Golf 42–4
    Spelling Ping-Pong 44–6
    Superstitions 167–9
    The Kluge 181–4
    We've Got Talent 159–61
    Who Am I? 221–3
general knowledge 11, 102
    Black 115–18
    Circus 128–30
    Dodo 118–21
    Pirates 106–9
    Stunts 134–7
    Sweets 131–4
    Trees 121–5
    UFOs (Unidentified Flying Objects) 109–11
    Water 125–7
    Yellow 111–15
Genre 18, 32–5
grammar 13
    Diamante Poetry 231–3
    Which Way? 294–7
Green Screen 273–4
group learning 9, 101, 157–8
    Be a Script Writer 64–6
    Celebrity 'Mastermind' 152–4
    Music and Lyrics 9, 20–2
    Self-Portrait 162–4
    Share for Success – 'Helping Me, Helping You' 157–9

Snippets and More 62–4
We've Got Talent 159–61

home and school activities 190, 289
    Just Breathe 300–1
    Metro Paper 297–9
    North, South, East, West 292–4
    Shades of Colours 290–2
    Which Way? 294–7

Idioms 226–9
imagination 10
    Be a Script Writer 64–6
    Creative Writing Pockets 66–8
    Rubber Band – A Writing Prompt 68–70
    We've Got Talent 159–61
    Who Am I? 221–3
incidental learning 194, 236
    Circus 128–30
    Dodo 118–21
    Framing 194–6
    Water 125–7
independent learning 11, 145, 256, 247
    Annotation 256–8
    Questioning Questions 247–50
    Volcanoes 145–8
Information Leaflet 35–8
information processing 10
Inspiration 266–70
investigative skills 11, 12, 118, 121
    Stunts 1347
    Superstitions 167–9
    Trees 121–5
    What We Eat 236–8
iTunes 274–5

Just Breathe 300–1

Keys 94–7
Kim's Game 174–6
Kluge, The 181–4
Knots 258–60

leaflets 35, 246
    Information Leaflet 35–8
learning 12, 101–3
    transferring learning across the curriculum 189–90
learning, cross-curricular 189–90
    Annotation 256–8
    Badge-Making 245–7
    Dewey Decimal System 238–40
    Film 260–2
    FreeRice 253–5
    Knots 258–60
    Questioning Questions 247–50
    Sounds 251–3
    Spinneracy 241–3
    Using the Whole Brain 243–5
    What We Eat 236–8

Letters, Words and Sentences 25–7
List the Lists 172–4
listening skills 251
    Sounds 251–3
literacy 10, 11, 17–18
Local Language 18, 78–80

maths 189–90, 191
    Armchair Olympics 200–2
    City Trip 203–5
    Design a Den 208–10
    Ellipse 192–4
    Framing 194–6
    Overseas Trip 205–8
    Visual Spatial 197–9
memory 10, 22, 102, 189–90, 191
    Celebrity 'Mastermind' 152–4
    Kim's Game 174–6
    List the Lists 172–4
    Nato Phonetic Alphabet 22–5
    Pelmanism 178–80
    Picture Card Prompts 176–8
    Smells 184–7
    The Kluge 181–4
Metro Paper 297–9
multi-sensory activities 9, 190
    Annotation 256–8
    Bananas 71–3
    Birds 278–80
    Film 260–2
    Kim's Game 174–6
    Tunnock's Teacake 73–5
    Verbs Charade 219–21
    Who Am I? 221–3
    Word Wheel 88–90
Music and Lyrics 20–2

Nato Phonetic Alphabet 22–5
newspapers 35
North, South, East, West 292–4
nouns 13, 94
    Diamante Poetry 231–3
    Nouns – Flashcards 90–2
number work 189–90, 191

observational skills 68, 150
Opposites 229–31
organising skills 10
    City Trip 203–5
    List the Lists 172–4
    Overseas Trip 205–8
overlearning 9–10, 25, 49, 102, 289
    'A' is for... 84–5
    Keys 94–7
    Spelling Corks 40–2
    Target Words and Visual Connections 49–50
    Word Wheel 88–90
Overseas Trip 205–8

paragraph writing 64
    Be a Script Writer 64–6
parts of speech 51, 219, 241
    Spinneracy 241–3
    Syllables, Syllables, Syllables 51–3
Peer, L. 226
Pelmanism 178–80
phonological processing 10, 20, 46, 49
physics 197
Picture Card Prompts 176–8
Pictures Say 100 Words 156–7
Pirates 106–9
Poetry Path 85–8
posters 35, 79
practical activities
    Badge-Making 245–7
    Birds 278–80
    Design a Den 208–10
    Framing 194–6
    Knots 258–60
    Metal 282–5
    Volcanoes 145–8
prepositions 214, 294
    PT (Position and Time) Prepositions 214–17
    Which Way? 294–7
prompts 10, 30, 71, 78, 106
    Black 115–18
    Creative Writing Pockets 66–8
    Picture Card Prompts 176–8
    Rubber Band – A Writing Prompt 68–70
punctuation 76–8
    Nouns – Flashcards 90–2

Questioning Questions 247–50
Quizzes 164–6

reading 17–18
    All about the Horse 27–9
    Genre 18, 32–5
    Information Leaflet 35–8
    Letters, Words and Sentences 25–7
reading: Metro Paper 297–9
    Music and Lyrics 20–2
    Nato Phonetic Alphabet 22–5
    Pirates 106–9
    Reading for Purpose 17, 30–2
    shared reading 27
Reid, G. 30, 226
relaxation 300
    Just Breathe 300–1
Review the Apps 275–8
rhyme 20, 169, 199, 257
    Music and Lyrics 20–2
rhythm 20, 87, 253
Rubber Band – A Writing Prompt 68–70

schema 12, 56, 64, 80, 102, 224, 268
Scrabble 25
script writing 64–6

self-esteem 10, 102–3
  Self-Portrait 162–4
  Share for Success – 'Helping Me, Helping You'
      157–9
  We've Got Talent 159–61
sensory awareness 68
sentence writing 64
  Be a Script Writer 64–6
sequencing 10, 11, 22, 62, 162, 198, 246
  Badge-Making 245–7
  Nato Phonetic Alphabet 22–5
  Self-Portrait 162–4
  Snippets and More 62–4
Shades of Colours 290–2
Share for Success – 'Helping Me, Helping You' 157–9
Smells 184–7
Snippets and More 62–4
songs 20, 34, 102, 114, 115, 144, 238
  Music and Lyrics 20–2
sounds 20
  Letters, Words and Sentences 25–7
  Sounds 251–3
spatial awareness 10
  Visual Spatial 197–9
spelling 10, 18
  spell checkers 18
  Spelling – Be a Teacher 46–9
  Spelling Corks 18, 40–2
  Spelling Golf 18, 42–4
  Spelling Ping-Pong 18, 44–6
  Syllables, Syllables, Syllables 51–3
  Target Words and Visual Connections 49–50
Spinneracy 241–3
sports 197
stress 10
Stunts 134–7
Summaries 280–2
Superstitions 167–9
Sweets 131–4
Syllables, Syllables, Syllables 51–3

Target Words and Visual Connections 49–50
Taste Texts 92–4
team building 20, 102
  Badge-Making 245–7
  Music and Lyrics 20–2
  The Kluge 181–4
technology 190
  Green Screen 273–4
  Metal 282–5
  Visual Spatial 197–9
Telephone/Mobile 285–7
Texthelp Read 18
Time 142–5
time-keeping difficulties 10
Tongue Twisters 97–9
Trees 121–5
Tunnock's Teacake 73–5

UFOs (Unidentified Flying Objects) 109–11
Use My Name 217–19
Using the Whole Brain 243–5

VANs (Verbs, Adjectives and Nouns) 13, 94
verbs 13, 94
  Diamante Poetry 231–3
  Time 142–5
  Verbs Charade 219–21
Visual Spatial 197–9
visual spelling techniques 47
  Spelling – Be a Teacher 46–9
  Target Words and Visual Connections 49–50
vocabulary development 13–14, 17, 18
  'A' is for... 84–5
  Bananas 71–3
  Be a Script Writer 64–6
  Forest Walk 18, 80–2
  Keys 94–7
  Nouns – Flashcards 90–2
  Pictures Say 100 Words 156–7
  Poetry Path 85–8
  Quizzes 164–6
  Rubber Band – A Writing Prompt 68–70
  Snippets and More 62–4
  Taste Texts 92–4
  Tongue Twisters 97–9
  VCOP (Vocabulary, Connectives, openers,
      Punctuation 76–8
  We've Got Talent 159–61
  Which Way? 294–7
  Word Wheel 88–90
Volcanoes 145–8

Water 125–7
We've Got Talent 159–61
West, T.G. 10, 266
What We Eat 236–8
What's New/Interesting/Forgettable? 140–1
Which Way? 294–7
Who Am I? 221–3
Wilson, Ros 76
Word Wheel 88–90
Write Gold™ 18
written expression 18
  Bananas 71–3
  Be a Script Writer 64–6
  Churchill 56–9
  Creative Writing Pockets 66–8
  Forest Walk 18, 80–2
  Frame It 60–2
  Local Language 18, 78–80
  PT (Position and Time) Prepositions 214–17
  Rubber Band – A Writing Prompt 68–70
  Snippets and More 62–4
  Tunnock's Teacake 18, 73–5
  VCOP (Vocabulary, Connectives, openers,
      Punctuation 76–8
  see also expressive writing

Yellow 111–15

About the Authors

Gavin Reid is an international practitioner psychologist with almost 40 years' experience in education and specifically in the field of dyslexia. Previously a classroom teacher and university lecturer, he has written a number of master's courses on dyslexia. He is widely published in the field of dyslexia and learning, and currently lectures worldwide. He has regular assessment consultancies in seven countries. Dr Reid is Chair of the British Dyslexia Association Accreditation Board and has sat on government panels on assessment and dyslexia, and has been engaged in a number of United Nations funded projects as a learning difficulties expert. His website is www.drgavinreid.com.

Nick Guise has years of practical experience as a specialist teacher for specific learning difficulties (SpLDs) with secondary school pupils. He has also worked with primary school children, and in alternative education, providing support to pupils across all year groups. Over a period of years, he has developed innovative teaching strategies to help pupils to access their strengths, so that they can build their confidence and progress in their studies. He has accumulated a range of evidence-based study techniques and life skills, and has taught through art-based work, music and multi-sensory projects. This approach has proved to be very effective in one-to-one and small-group settings. Memory development has been a major factor in his work, and a variety of fun-based and memorable activities has led to improved confidence in pupils and the development of skills that could be transferred to help them in learning and revising.

Jennie Guise has extensive experience of assessing for specific learning difficulties. She has authored and co-authored a number of articles and books on the topic of assessment and barriers to learning. She has presented internationally at conferences and in workshops for teachers and parents. She has taught a wide range of students, has worked in research, and now works in applied practice as founder and Director of DysGuise Ltd (www.dysguise.com). Dr Guise's main interests are in identifying what will help individual learners to progress, and in working collaboratively with educators, parents and carers to apply that knowledge in practical ways.